Those
Nut-cracking Elizabethans

PLATE I

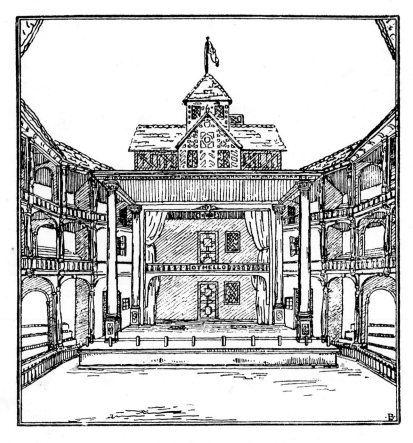

A Typical Elizabethan Public Theatre

THOSE
NUT-CRACKING ELIZABETHANS

STUDIES OF THE
EARLY THEATRE AND DRAMA

BY

W. J. LAWRENCE

Author of *The Life of Gustavus Vaughan Brooke,*
Shakespeare's Workshop,
etc., etc.

LONDON
THE ARGONAUT PRESS
1935

PRINTED IN GREAT BRITAIN

To

SIR JOHN MARTIN-HARVEY
in the (perhaps vain) hope that these studies
will give him a tithe of the pleasure that
his *Œdipus* and *Sydney Carton*
have given me

PREFACE

Now that the bell has rung for the last lap in a long life of ardent seeking after the solutions to many mysteries, I am warned to enter betimes upon a course of stocktaking with the view of determining what among the host of my scattered writings can be justifiably snatched from Oblivion's maw. A difficult task, this sifting, for a good deal more than mere chaff has to be discarded. As tiller of the ploughed lands as well as of virgin soil, it is the business of the historical investigator to eradicate the weeds of Fallacy, no matter how gorgeously coloured, and to make two facts grow where only one grew before. Nothing of his that fails to achieve one or other of these aims or to contribute materially towards that end is worthy of preservation. Accordingly, self-criticism in these matters must be vigilant, for it is with most writers as with most mothers, the weaklings of the brood are apt to be the best beloved. I can only hope, therefore, that in selecting for preservation the present sheaf of Elizabethan studies I have nowhere shown any undue partiality.

To the proprietors of *The Fortnightly Review*, *The Criterion*, *The Dublin Magazine*, *Life and Letters*, *The Sackbut*, *The Times Literary Supplement*, *The New Statesman and Nation*, and *The Stage*, in whose publications these studies originally appeared, I tender my best thanks for so graciously permitting me to reproduce them. It needs to say, however, that all have been revised and one or two rewritten and expanded beyond recognition. The illustrations are new.

Nor must I omit to express my gratitude to my old friend Dr S. A. Tannenbaum of New York for his kindness in allowing me to use as a frontispiece his scientific reconstruction of a typical Elizabethan Public Theatre, already published in America, a design in which I have a sort of paternal interest inasmuch as some of the details are based on my own personal researches.

W. J. L.

February 1935

CONTENTS

LIST OF ILLUSTRATIONS

Chapter I

THOSE NUT-CRACKING
ELIZABETHANS

Life has always been streaked with minor ironies. It is curious to note how, time and again throughout the seventeenth century, the players, in their endeavours to propitiate and stabilise their supporters, so often made rods for their own backs. Concessions were apt to act as boomerangs, and not even the creature comforts of the audience could be attended to without some jarring rebound. When Paul Hentzner, the Brandenburg jurist, visited London in 1598 and went the round of the theatres, he was struck by the custom of hawking apples, pears and nuts in the house while the audience was slowly assembling. To that practice there does not seem at the first glance to be any possible objection, but, unfortunately, the Elizabethan playgoer of the commoner order got into a habit of persistent nut-cracking which proved a nuisance. True, it was not a neurotic age, and (to adapt Johnson's retort to Garrick) Punch was not expected to have any particular feelings; but, all the same, we have abundant testimony of the annoyance occasioned not only to the players but to concentrative playgoers by the nut-cracker. He became the symbol of those "barren spectators" for whom my lord Hamlet expressed such high contempt. Not that the habit was confined to men alone: both sexes indulged in it. In 1601, at a time when rank personal satire in play and poem was all the rage, Tucca, in Dekker's *Satiromastix*, complained to Horace that "a gentleman or an honest citizen shall not sit in your pennie-bench theatres, with his squirrel by his side cracking nuts, nor sneake into a taverne with his mermaid, but he shall be satyr'd and epigramm'd upon, and his humour must run upo' th' stage".

Here, however, we have merely a plain statement of fact; it is not until a trifle over a decade later that a note of objurgation concerning the habit is sounded. Holding forth in defence of his companions, Young Loveless, in Beaumont and Fletcher's *The Scornful Lady*, says:

> ...These are no rav'ning footmen,
> No fellows that at ordinaries dare eat
> Their eighteenpence out before they rise,
> And yet go hungry to a play, and crack
> More nuts than would suffice a dozen squirrels:
> Besides the din, which is most damnable.
> I had rather rail, and be confined to a boat-maker
> Than link among such rascals.

In another play of about the same period (1615), by the same authors, there is a similar contemptuous allusion to nut-cracking. In *Wit Without Money*, Valentine showers invective on the heads of his fickle friends, and bids them continue in their littleness and ignorance:

> Till you break in at plays, like 'prentices
> For three a groat, and crack nuts with the scholars
> In penny rooms again.

It is remarkable that on this score Ben Jonson, otherwise so vehement in his correction of abuses, should have remained so long silent, but, in 1625, he too raised his voice in disapproval. Listen to what he says in the Court prologue to *The Staple of News*:

> A work not smelling of the lamp, to-night,
> But fitted for your Majesty's disport,
> And writ to the meridian of your Court,
> We bring; and hope it may produce delight,
> The rather being offered as a rite,
> To scholars that can judge, and fair report
> The sense they hear, above the vulgar sort
> Of nut-crackers, that only come for sight.

Since rare old Ben's comedy had been originally produced before the select audience of the Blackfriars, where it was equivocally received, there is somewhat of a hint here that the Jacobean gallant had acquired a playhouse habit that in earlier days had been confined to commoner folk. Later evidence turns suspicion into certainty. It comes from a dramatist of a certain curious type which Jonson and his class, for very good reasons, abominated.

With the view of gaining effective dramatic illustration of the sublimities arising from the old-new cult of platonic love, Queen Henrietta, in Caroline days, encouraged sundry courtiers inflicted with the itch of writing (not to speak of a handful of aspiring young University men) to indite plays for the especial delectation and enjoyment of the Court. After these had been duly acted at Whitehall, it was the custom of this superior-minded brood of amateurs, in order that their plays might reach a wider public, to give them free, gratis and for nothing to the players. They had no desire, however, to be classed with the Shirleys and Bromes of the hour, and when their pieces were publicly presented, took care to warn the spectators they were not of that common sort of clay that wrote for money. Thus, when Jasper Mayne's comedy, *The City Match*, after having been given at Court, was brought out at the Blackfriars in 1639, the author began his prologue, most impertinently, by informing the spectators that the fortunes of the play by no means depended on their suffrages, since it had been written at the behest of the King:

Yet he to the King's command needs the King's writ
To keep him safe, not to be arraign'd for wit.
Not that he fears his name can suffer wrack
From them who sixpence pay and sixpence crack,
To such he wrote not.

The reference here is to those "magistrates of wit", the stage stoolholders, who, after paying an extra sixpence for their seats, expended another in nuts. This latter disbursement, viewing the fact that money then had five or six times its present purchasing power, points not only to the extravagance of the times but to vile profiteering, and indicates why the players so long tolerated the nuisance of nut-cracking. Profiteering, indeed, can be proved in a more satisfactory way. In his *Picturae Loquentes*, which fell from the press in 1631, Wye Saltonstall has a character portrait of "A Lawyer's Clerke", in which he tells us that, "at a new play he'll be sure to be seen in the threepenny room, and buyes his pippins before he goes in, because he can have more for his money".

In the old days, apparently, few could sit out any sort of amusement without munching something between-whiles. (In that respect, we have not wholly spent our heritage.) Even Pepys while at the play, careful man as he was, gave a fancy price for his oranges. As for nut-cracking in earlier times, there were no places of amusement where it was not pursued. Do we not find Shave'em, the prostitute, saying in Massinger's Caroline comedy of *The City Madam*?—

You would have me foot it,
To the Dancing of the Ropes, sit a whole afternoon there
In expectation of nuts and pippins;
Gape round about me, and yet not find a chapman
That, in courtesy, will bid a chop of mutton
Or a pint of drum wine for me.

One recalls how Sir Thomas Palmer, in his lines in memory of John Fletcher prefixed to the Beaumont and Fletcher folio of 1647, wrote:

I could praise Heywood now; or tell how long
Falstaff from cracking nuts hath kept the throng:
But for a Fletcher I must take an age.

No doubt that reference to the fat knight's compelling powers was intended as a testimony to Shakespeare's genius, but there was a brilliant Caroline poet who thought that nothing but the lowest of low comedy could paralyse the jaws of the nut-crackers. Once, in expressing his contempt for those who wrote down to the level of the groundlings, Tom Randolph characterised them as indulging in

    ...the nonsense of the constables,
Such jig-like flim-flams being got to make
The rabble laugh, and nut-cracking forsake.[1]

[1] Randolph's *Works*, ed. Hazlitt, II, p. 514.

What clownery could do, the best of music was powerless to effect; between the acts, to make up for lost time the nut-crackers set their jaws to work with redoubled energy. Remark what Gayton says on the subject in his poem on *The Art of Longevity*, published in 1659, but written a score of years earlier:

In Hazel-nut, or Filbert, cold and dry
Of temper, doth a windy moisture lye
Which yields but little nourishment, so rough
It will not pass the stomach soon enough,
But lies like a bullet, or small shot of lead,
Yet upon these the vulgar sort do feed,
And at the Playhouses, betwixt the Acts,
The Musick Room is drown'd with these nut-cracks.

It is notable that when at the Restoration the masses had lost their way to the theatre, nuts and apples went out and oranges came in. There was little in which the dominance of the Puritan had occasioned so much sundering with the past as in matters of playgoing custom and theatrical routine. In his desire for suppression, he had only succeeded in bringing about a material improvement. Every age pursues the silly habit of despising its predecessor, and we can judge of the lofty contempt entertained by the Restoration wits for their forbears by a reflection which occurs in the prologue to Corye's play, *The Generous Enemies*, as delivered at the Theatre Royal in 1671:

> I cannot choose but laugh when I look back and see
> The strange vicissitudes of poetrie,
> Your aged fathers came to plays for wit,
> And sat knee-deep in nutshells in the pit;
> Coarse hangings then, instead of scenes, were worn
> And Kidderminster did the stage adorn.

The astonishing thing is that, notwithstanding the latter part of this reflection and what has been said about the subject it discusses by Flecknoe and other of the writer's contemporaries, there are scholars of sterling ability who still maintain that scenery was in regular use in some of the old Caroline theatres when Puritan ascendancy brought about their downfall.

Chapter II

SHAKESPEARE'S USE OF ANIMALS

Though latter-day research in the course of its steady progress has extirpated a good many old fallacies concerning the Elizabethan drama and its presentation, it has not as yet been forceful enough to penetrate beyond the outworks of that secluded type of scholarship which stubbornly persists in looking upon Shakespeare as a law unto himself, a phenomenon to be examined in a vacuum. Progress has been delayed by ill-directed assaults on these pregnable strongholds. The time has come for full recognition of the fact that there are no arbitrary solutions to Shakespearian problems, and that such as remain intractable can be determined only by severely logical deduction from a premiss of newly acquired data. Remarkably enough, though Elizabethan investigators abound, there are vital matters concerning Shakespeare's theatrical environment which still call for clear demonstration; and it will be found, I think, that one group of little-known facts, once they are properly marshalled, yield us the answer to a couple of Shakespearian riddles regarding which more or less idle speculation has long been rife. The question whether horses were ridden on to the stage in the early performances of *Macbeth*, and the further question whether a real bear was pressed into service on the first production of *The Winter's Tale*: these admit of no solution running counter to the stage customs of the time in regard to the use and representation of quadrupeds. What I propose doing now is to educe the principles pursued in this respect by the Elizabethan players, and, by force of their authority, answer the two questions.

There can be little doubt that Shakespeare's public had a peculiar liking for the sight of animals on the stage, a liking much greater than has been evinced by any public since, and that that partiality was very extensively gratified. But, as a rule, only such quadrupeds were utilised in drama as could be led— and led illusively—on to the stage: one good reason why in cases where there is no indication of the animal being under control, we are justified in suspecting that it was of the imitation order. Kine and sheep and deer were taboo. But we must call to mind that constant as was the striving after realism in early stage representation, realism imposed no limits. Where the actuality could not be shown the audience contentedly accepted its symbol. In its simplicity of mind, Shakespeare's public could do what we cannot—view an imitation lion or bear in high tragedy with wholly serious eyes. To-day, we are all Peter Bells, and the sight of such simulacra under such conditions would irresistibly remind us of the buffooneries of Christmas pantomime.

In Shakespeare's day, the art of property-animal making was by no means in its primitive stage. As many old Revels parchments attest, deft modelling of the sort had been practised at Court in association with the gorgeous indoor pageants which first began to be given in the reign of Henry VII. When one seeks an indication of the capacity of the Elizabethan stage property-makers in this respect, one finds it in the frequent use in Chronicle Histories of dummy heads in decapitation scenes. A condemned person-age went off to the block, and immediately his gory head would be brought in. No stock property would have answered all the requirements: women suffered by the axe as well as men. A head had to be made in correspondence with the lineaments, com-plexion and hair of the victim. Concerning the early stage use of property animals, we are not, as it happens, left wholly to speculation, since we know from Philip Henslowe's inventory that among the properties belonging to the Admiral's Men in 1598 were one lion, two lions' heads, a lion's skin, a bear's skin, a boar's head and a black dog. Later indications show that there were practically no limitations to the skill of the early seventeenth-century property-maker. In Davenport's comedy, *The City Night Cap*, as produced at the Cockpit in 1624, a masque was introduced in which a stag, a ram, a bull and a goat danced. Some six years previously, when Jonson's masque, *For the Honour of Wales*, was given its second performance at Court, it comprised a quaint dance of Welsh goats. Real goats, it is to be noted, were seldom introduced into ordinary stage plays. As in the case of the monkey (who, in his live state, put in a solitary appearance in *Eastward Hoe* in 1605), I can recall only one example. In Heywood's *If You Know not me, You Know no bodie*, Part I, an order is gravely given for a prisoner to be brought in, and the Clown springs one of his jokes by leading in a nanny. Animals, whether real or imitative, were mostly introduced for comic purposes, but the king of beasts was taken in deadly seriousness until Shakespeare burlesqued his stage ectype in *A Midsummer Night's Dream*. In the anonymous and slightly earlier tragedy of *Locrine*, the action opens with a symbolical dumb show, duly explained by a Presenter, in which a lion chases a bear and is shot by an archer.

The dog (breed immaterial and mongrels not excluded) was easily the most popular of all early stage animals, just as the cat ranked among the least seen, and that despite the fact that grimalkin was the pioneer quadruped of the secular English drama. One recalls how Hodge, in that most primitive of native comedies, *Gammer Gurton's Needle*, thinks, in his bewilderment, that the much sought for needle is in Gib the cat's throat, and how narrow an escape she had from an ignominious death. But, on the Elizabethan stage proper, and as a purely domestic animal—the reason for the distinction will appear later—puss rarely got an innings. With precautionary tact, a cat is brought in in a bag in *Every Man Out of His Humour*, and one also figures in a much later play, Sampson's *The Vow Breaker*, presently to be discussed.

Shakespeare was not given to repeating himself, and he only once made comic capital out of a dog. For Launce's rebukings of the misbehaving Crab there was mild precedent, inasmuch as in *Sir Clyomon and Clamydes*, a popular piece of romantic fustian which dates from about 1578, Coryn the shepherd comes on with his dog and threatens to beat him. But, in this case as in all others, Shakespeare never borrowed an idea without bettering it. Whether the introduction of Crab was simply *à la mode*, or whether the scenes in which he figured enjoyed such vogue as to influence other dramatists, the fact remains that in and about the period of *The Two Gentlemen of Verona*, much play with dogs was made on the stage. In 1597, in the fifth act of Munday's *Downfall of Robert Earl of Huntingdon*, the Jailor of Nottingham led on a dog, in accord with textual requirements. Shortly afterwards popular sport was exemplified in *Histriomastix*, a mystifying play in which Velure and Lyon-rash, when about to go duck-hunting, arrive on the scene with a water-spaniel and a duck. This incident, with more than one dog, was repeated some years later in a highly successful Fortune play called *The Roaring Girl*. In *The Merry Devil of Edmonton*, the instincts of a hound are deftly availed of to lead to the accidental discovery of Millicent in the obscurity of the wood. But the only play of the period in which a dog is made part of the weft of the plot is Jonson's *Every Man Out of His Humour*, in which we are introduced to Puntarvolo's absorption in his domestic animals, a dog and a cat, both of which he purposes taking with him to Constantinople to win a wager, and might have gained the coveted odds of five to one, had not Macilente poisoned his dog.

Most early stage dogs were led on by somebody, but there is one remarkable exception. It occurs in a curious scene in the last act of Jonson's *The Staple of News*, a Blackfriars production of 1625, where the

insanity of Pennyboy senior is revealed by his
putting his two dogs Block and Lollard on trial by
due process of law for certain offences which recall
Crab's ill-bred habits. The dogs are catechised by
him, called forth alternately by name, and as often
dismissed. How was it done? Can it have been that
the dogs were the property and companions of the
player of Pennyboy senior, and given their real
names? If not, it is puzzling to know how they
were taught to take their cues. It is noteworthy, by
the way, that about a decade later, William Sampson
rang the changes on this quaint trial scene in his
tragedy of *The Vow Breaker*. In the third act of the
play, Joshua the Puritan comes on with a cat on a
string, said cat being in dire disgrace for having
caught a mouse on a Sunday. In the trial that
ensues, Joshua figures as prosecuting counsel, judge,
and even jury: nay more, he is about to turn hang-
man, when Gray cries, "Stay, stay, a pardon, a
pardon".

   Besides the many real live dogs and a few real live
cats, the Elizabethan audience was regaled on occasion with the sight—and sometimes a good deal
more than the sight—of dogs and cats of a super-
natural, and, therefore (paradoxically enough),
manufactured order. The "one black dog" listed by
Henslowe among the Admiral's Men's properties in

1598 belongs to this category, and might have been provided for an earlier dramatisation of the grim old legend on which *The Black Dog of Newgate*, a play in two parts written by four authors for Worcester's Men in 1602, was based. But perhaps this is an idle guess, seeing that a black dog was usually the familiar of the early stage witch. It was as such that one figured prominently in *The Witch of Edmonton*, a Cockpit production of 1621. Tom-boy, as Mother Sawyer affectionately called him, was evidently a water-spaniel, and, though capable of barking on occasion, not only had the gift of speech, but was learned in the Latin tongue. Half demon, half dog, he now and again evinced the canine delight in frolic, finding a congenial companion in Cuddy Banks, and he once obliged by playing the fiddle to provide the music for a morris dance. Towards the close of this curiously piebald play, his coat turns white, thus signifying to the witch that her hour has come. But for a dog of brains and enterprise, Tom-boy might have been expected to be a trifle more original. His principal feat was a shameless usurpation of puss's prerogative, as the immortal nursery rhyme, "Hey diddle diddle", testifies. It had been legitimately performed in the opening act of Middleton's *The Witch*, at that juncture where Hecate indulges in certain conjurations, and the cat enters playing on a fiddle. Later on she was to descend from above and burst into song, warbling "a brave treble in her own language", a rare example of melodious caterwauling which was ultimately to be transferred with the play's other musico-spectacular adornments to a revision of *Macbeth*. Thus it was that Shakespeare, while despising cats, had (in his own lifetime) a cat thrust upon him. Not that he had any serious objection to property animals, for, about the time that his great tragedy was thus maltreated, he cheerfully utilised at least four property dogs—spirits "in the shape of hounds"—in the scene in *The Tempest* where Caliban and Stephano and Trinculo are coursed.

Although wholly unvenerated, the ass is the most venerable of all stage quadrupeds, and enjoys the distinction of being the first beast to be given a speaking part. (A prognostic surely of the coming diffusion of English.) We find him figuring in the old Chester miracle play of *Balak and Balaam*, wherein he was called upon to deliver a melancholy pleading speech of some fourteen lines. A sham in the beginning, he has remained for the most part a sham ever since. His appearances on the Elizabethan stage were few and far between, and, so far as can be determined, he does not seem to have ever been seen there in the flesh. Considerable ingenuity was exercised early in the seventeenth century in counterfeiting him, since it is on record that Silenus in *The Masque of Flowers*, as given at Court on Twelfth Night, 1614, was mounted "upon an artificial ass, which sometimes being taken with the strain of the music, did bow down his ears, and listen with great attention". But what was done in the old miracle plays and the lavish Court masques had no particular bearing on the regular stage, and, in the absence of direct evidence, we are left to speculate as to the method of ass representation in the Elizabethan theatre. Neddy, as beast of burden, fulfilled his normal office in *Summer's Last Will and Testament*, but Nash's delightfully fanciful play never seems to have had public performance, since the only known representation of it was the one given by boys at a Croydon mansion in 1592. No orthodox stage could then have been provided, for Bacchus, on making his entry on a donkey having trappings of ivy, calls out, "one of you hold my ass while I light: walk him up and down the hall, till I talk a word or two". There is nothing really to show whether the wine-god's mount was of the live or the imitative order, but it is interesting to note that in an anonymous play printed in that very same year, *The Tragedye of Solyman and Perseda*, an artificial ass seems to have figured. Piston's skittish

charger had evidently suffered in the wars, as he had
lost his tail and had had his ears cropped and his nose
slit, but he was still possessed of a devil and prone to
throw his rider, should any liberties be taken with
him. This play, too, judging by its directions, seems
to have been acted on the floor of a hall. A third
ass-piece of the period, *The Contention of Liberality
and Prodigality*—the only one known to have been
acted publicly—was revived in 1601, and acted at
Court by boy-players. In this a poor little donkey,
lean as Rosinante, was brought on in several scenes.
Tenacity, who makes his first entrance riding upon
him, is described by the Postilion as "a lubber, fat,
great and tall, upon a tired ass, bare, short and
small". Hardly, one should say, a real animal. It is
to be noted, however, that there is virtually only one
extant common-theatre play of the Elizabethan era
in which an ass has a place, Daborne's *A Christian
Turn'd Turk*, an unsuccessful piece printed in 1612
without indication of the producing company or
the place of performance. In a dumb show in this,
representing the reception of Ward the pirate into
the Turkish faith, the apostate rides in on an ass,
dismounts for the ceremony, and then departs in the
manner in which he came.

It is possible that in a very few cases a real ass was
used, but, admitting so much, the logic of the situa-

tion is that, if an animal of such comparative small-
ness, so stolid and controllable, was so rarely pressed
into stage service, it is hardly rational to infer on the
slenderest of evidence that the horse, a highly
nervous animal, apt, as we know, to lash out with
his heels when he hears them rattle on the boards,
would have received more employment. Let us not
forget that in Elizabethan days the stage was encumbered with spectators. Shakespeare is surely
the best authority on this subject. Did he not make
Chorus in *King Henry V* ask the audience to "piece
out our imperfections with your thoughts" and

> Think, when we talk of horses, that you see them
> Printing their proud hoofs i' the receiving earth.

There are many situations in the old Chronicle
Histories where the action positively demanded the
presence of horses had it been in anywise customary
to bring horses on the stage, but it is significant that
neither in the text of these plays nor of any play
printed in Shakespeare's lifetime do we get the
slightest indication of the use of horses. Note how
neatly their absence is accounted for in the field-of-
battle scene in 2 *Henry VI*, act v, sc. 2. The joke of
the thing, however, is that, extravagant as is the lip
worship they give him, Shakespeare's authority to
speak of Shakespeare has not proved of sufficient

certitude to prevent many literal-minded followers
of Halliwell-Phillipps from pinning their faith to
the *ipse dixit* of Simon Forman the astrologer. It is
true that Forman kept a book of memoranda concerning plays that he had seen, but it needs to bear
in mind for what purpose he kept the book.[1] He
entitled it "The Booke of Plaies and Notes therof
per Formans for pollicie". His aim in keeping it was
to extract from the plays he visited whatever rules
for the pursuit of strategy and tactics in the rough
and tumble of life they embodied. Since the action
of a piece was for him a minor concern, he contented
himself in giving a summary of its plot. Having
seen a performance of *Macbeth* at the Globe on
April 20, 1610, he began his account of it with:

there was to be observed firste how Macbeth and
Banko two noblemen of Scotland ridinge thorow a
wood, there stode before them three women fairies or
nimphs, and saluted Macbeth, etc. etc.

On the strength of this statement, the literalists so
far dogmatise as to postulate the common use of
horses on the Elizabethan stage, but, assuming that

[1] Since this was written that sturdy iconoclast, Dr S. A. Tannenbaum of New York, has unhesitatingly denounced the Forman
manuscript as a forgery (*Shakespearian Scraps*, pp. 1–35). It
certainly presents elements of suspicion, but while two opinions
are still held upon the point, I prefer to take no chances, and
proceed on the assumption that the book is genuine.

the text of the first act of the tragedy is identical with
the text as Forman heard it, nothing could be easier
than to show the absurdity of the inference. The
wood existed only in Forman's imagination, for the
scene of action turns out to be a blasted heath, and
the horses were equally imaginary. Suppose we
assume, despite the absence of all indications to that
effect, that Macbeth and Banquo really were on
horseback, and remained so throughout the scene.
If it were necessary to show them mounted in order
to indicate that they were journeying across country,
by a parity of reasoning it was likewise necessary for
Ross and Angus to come on about the middle of the
scene in the same way, more especially as they all
depart together. What point could there have been
in Chorus's plea in *King Henry V*, if four horses could
have been congregated on the stage in this way?

But there is a solution to the mystery. Passing
strange is it that it has never struck anybody that
Macbeth and Banquo might have walked on the
stage on making their first appearance, and yet
subtly and silently conveyed to Forman or any
other tolerably experienced playgoer that they were
travelling on horseback. We do not know how they
were then garbed, but what we do know is that
there was in those days a certain conventional
method of signifying that a character was about to

go on a journey or was in the midst of one, a method still pursued in post-Restoration days. Examples of the convention abound, but a couple belonging to different periods may be cited. In *Look About You*, at the beginning is the direction, "Enter Robert Hood, a young nobleman, a servant with him, with riding wands in their hands, as if they had been new-lighted". Hood bids his servant "Go walk the horses, wait me on the hill", and, later on, when about to depart, cries, "Holla, there—my horse". So, too, in Chapman's *Revenge of Bussy D'Ambois*, a play of a decade later, one notes that in the middle of the fourth act the captured Clermont is being taken by Maillard and a number of mounted men to the King. The scene opens in the midst of the journey, and they should all properly be on horse-back. Remark how that necessity was evaded without any marring of the illusion. The situation is clearly conveyed by Maillard's casual comment:

This pretty talking and our horses walking
Down this steep hill, spends time with equal profit.

Such is the frequency with which scenes of this type occur in Elizabethan drama that one would be disposed to say that horses were never brought on the stage until at least half a century after Shakespeare's death, were it not for the arresting circumstance that two early plays exist which seem to have required their employment. The first of these, *Thomas of Woodstock*, a Chronicle History, has come down to us solely in a manuscript prompt-book of the early Caroline period, and, although it is known to have been acted before 1616, we have absolutely no clue to the producing company or the place of performance. The second is Heywood's *The Late Lancashire Witches*, a Globe play of 1633. Act III, sc. 2 of *Thomas of Woodstock* is laid in the courtyard of Plashey. A servant announces the arrival of a horseman at the gate, and says he refuses to dismount until the gate be opened. Gloucester orders his admission. "Enter a spruce Courtier a horse-backe." He mistakes the Duke, owing to his customary plainness of garb, for a groom, and bids him walk his horse. Gloucester, with grim humour, does as he is told, and talks to the horse as he leads him about:

Come on, sir, you have sweat hard about this haste, yett I thinke you knowe little of the business. Why so I say; youre a very indifferent beast, you'le follow any man that will lead you. Now truly sir you looke but leanely on't; you feed not in Westminster Hall adays, where so many sheepe and oxen are devoured.... You knowe not the duke neither no more than your master, and yett you have as much witt as he. Ifaith, say a man should steal ye and feed ye fatter: could ye run away with him? Ah, your silence argues a consent I see.

There is no getting away from the fact that an actual horse was here used, a remarkable exception to the general rule, but the point is not so assured in connexion with *The Late Lancashire Witches*. In the fourth act of Heywood's play the noisy ceremony of the skimmington is performed. The stage direction reads: "Enter drum (beating before) a Skimmington and his wife on a horse". Both are at once rudely pulled off by the mob and beaten. Then comes another direction, "drum beats alarm—horse comes away", which may or may not mean that the horse runs off. Possibly, in this case, a property horse may have been used, though the supposition is not favoured by the fact that, apart from the hobby horse (which could have only one rider, the horse and the rider being one), we have no record of the early use of property horses.

Come we now to a consideration of the bear scene in *The Winter's Tale* and of the scholarly consensus regarding it. There is to-day pretty wide endorsement of the theory advanced some quarter of a century ago by Paul Monkemeyer, an able German investigator, to the effect that a tame bear was used at the Globe in the play and that it was borrowed for the nonce from the neighbouring

Bear Garden. Plausible as this sounds, it fails to bear examination. There were no tame bears in the old Bear Garden. Constant baiting had rendered them all ferocious. Few full-grown bears are to be trusted in an unmuzzled state, bruin being by nature treacherous, yet the bear that chased Antigonus came in free and undirected, and went off in a particular way as quickly as it came. One can imagine the panic that would have been created among the stoolholding gallants on the stage by the sudden appearance of a loose bear. Even if we admit that a tame animal of the sort could have been readily procured, we are compelled to ask ourselves what need was there to seek for it at a time when playgoers were accustomed to see property bears in situations both of a serious and a comic nature. The evidence of *Locrine* and other plays on the point cannot be ignored. Once a bowing to convention is conceded, a gratifying result follows, for by pursuing the train of thought we arrive by natural transition at the circumstances which influenced Shakespeare when he sought for a ready means of disposing of Antigonus. (It must be remembered that neither the bear nor his victim figures in Greene's romance of *Pandosto* on which Shakespeare based.) On Shrove Sunday, 1610, or only a few months before *The Winter's Tale* was produced by the King's Men, they had given a performance of the old play of *Muce-dorus* at Court, and, according to custom, had signalised its revival by some interpolations, notable among which was a new episode in the first act. This preceded the old scene in which Segasto enters just after having slain a marauding bear, with a sword in one hand and the bear's head in the other. In the addition, Mouse the clown comes on in hot haste to say he has just encountered a bear, making address to the audience in the old naïve way. He decides to go out backwards, so as not to be taken unawares should the beast approach, but bruin comes in the opposite direction, and poor Mouse, all unconscious of his contiguity, tumbles over him. Obviously, this was no tame bear from the Bear Garden, but a property animal. Puerile as this gratuitous piece of buffoonery sounds, it no doubt contributed to the success of the play when it was performed at the Globe at intervals during the next few months. (There were absolutely no "runs" in those days.) Somehow, Shakespeare, when scheming out *The Winter's Tale*, happened to think of that property bear, and at once the fate of the worthy Antigonus was relentlessly determined.

Chapter III

THE ELIZABETHAN PRIVATE PLAYHOUSE

It is matter of humiliation that, although for some time past Elizabethan research has been striding along in seven-leagued boots, there still remain one or two vital problems towards whose solution no satisfactory approach has been made. Paramount among these is the question of the early private playhouse, in what manner it was instituted, and how it contrived for long to rise superior to the law. If there has been bafflement on these points, it is not because the evidence is sparse or unsufficing, but for the more painful reason that seekers after the truth have gone off on a false scent and have been busily hunting after a wholly imaginary quarry. A recent discovery by an American scholar, Professor H. N. Hillebrand, reveals that the old institution, un-scientifically labelled in latter days as the Elizabethan Private Playhouse, dates from 1575,[1] but no further illumination can come until scholarship grasps the

[1] H. N. Hillebrand, *The Child Actors* (Urbana, 1926), Pt. I, pp. 123-4.

surprising fact that from that year for a quarter of
a century onwards no such thing was known as
a private playhouse or theatre. What it has been
stupidly doing is to read into that period terms
peculiar to Stuart times. The germ of what was
known early in the seventeenth century as a private
playhouse was always spoken of in its own day as
a "private house". This mild distinction is of vastly
greater importance than is apparent: so much so,
indeed, that in tracing the primary significance of
the earlier term, one goes more than halfway towards clearing up the entire mystery. What we first
require to note is that no use of the term "private
playhouse" can be found before 1606, when Dekker
employed it in his pamphlet on *The Seven Deadly
Sinnes of London*. Three years earlier, when the
Gilderstone of the spurious *Hamlet* quarto came to
speak of the defection of "the principall publike
audience" from the tragedians of the city, he did not
say that it had been lured away by a rival theatre,
but that it had "turned to private playes, and to the
humour of children". Sly, too, as we have him in
the special Globe induction of 1604 to Marston's
The Malcontent, knows only of one type of playhouse, and when asked to remove himself from sight,
accordingly protests, "why, we may sit upon the
stage at the private house". It would be idle to

pretend that he was here using an accidental term. In accord with the fact that labels with us have always had the mystifying trick of persisting long after the thing on which they were originally bestowed had so far changed as to nullify their fitness, we find sundry plays of the Caroline period (when no playhouse could have been accurately termed private save that of Whitehall) described on their title-pages as having been acted "at the private house in Drury Lane" or in the Blackfriars. It is furthermore noteworthy that in his prologue to *The Fawn*, a play produced at the Blackfriars in or about 1604, Marston elects to style the place of performance simply a room:

> But if the nimble form of comedy,
> Mere spectacle of life and public manners,
> May gracefully arrive to your pleased ears,
> We boldly dare the utmost death of fears;
> For we do know that this most fair-fill'd room
> Is loaden with most attic judgments, ablest spirits,
> Than whom there are none more exact, full, strong,
> Yet none more soft, benign in censuring.

How, then, was the original use of the term "private house" as applied to a regular playing-place, justified? No well-equipped stage historian requires to seek far for an answer. The term arose in a happy attempt to avail of the exceptions allowed in a restrictive city edict aimed against the players. Early in December 1574, when no theatres existed and the only public playing-places were the inn-yards, an Act of Common Council was issued to regulate acting and keep the number of players within bounds.[1] This made the innkeeper the re-sponsible person, and ordained that before acting could take place in his yard, he should give sureties for the preservation of good order and for the exclusion of the players during the time of plague and of divine service, the penalty for every in-fraction being a fine of £5. It was likewise decreed that a poor tax at a rate unspecified but arbitrarily determinable by the Lord Mayor and corporation be levied on the innkeeper; practically a tax on the receipts. Moreover, all new plays had to be licensed by a city censor. From this enactment there was only one loophole of escape:

Provydid allwaie that this Acte (otherwise then touching the publishinge of unchaste, sedycious, and vnmete matters) shall not extend to anie plaies, Enterludes, Comodies, Tragidies, or shewes to be played or shewed in the pryvate house, dwellinge, or lodging of anie nobleman, Citizen, or gentleman, which shall or will then have the same thear so played or shewed in his presence, for the festyvities of anie

[1] Cited *in extenso* by Chambers, *The Elizabethan Stage*, IV, pp. 273-6.

marriage, assemblye of ffrendes, or otherlyke cawse, withowte publique or comen collection of money of the auditorie, or behoulders theareof, referringe alwaie to the Lorde Maire and Aldermen for the tyme beinge the Iudgement, and construction accordinge to equitie, what shalbe counted such a playinge or shewinge in a pryvate place, anie thinge in this Acte to the Contrarie notwithstanding.

Following this came a more drastic order, due to sundry fulminations from the pulpit, which forbade all acting "in open spectacle" within city limits, but still permitting performances "in private houses only at Marriages or such like". The ultimate outcome of this persistent harrying of the players was the erection in 1576 on a site outside the city walls and beyond municipal control of Burbage's Theater, notable as the first permanent public playhouse. Meanwhile, however, the supply of acting not having proved equal to the demand, a project was conceived by a man of some note, unassociated with the players, of establishing (if only for a time) a new kind of playing-place without in anywise infringing upon the city ordinances. This was Sebastian Westcote, Master of the Children of St Paul's, a musician who for a score of years previously had been in the habit of utilising his choirboys in the giving of dramatic performances at Court before the Queen occasionally at Christmas, and who now saw a way of improving their histrionic technique by keeping them in constant practice, and incidentally of making a little extra money. What he conceived was the setting up of an amateur subscription theatre which should take full advantage of the permission to act in private allowed by the Act of Common Council of December 1574, without in anywise running counter to its main provisions. Patrons he had no difficulty in getting, since acting at Court had long been confined to Christmas and Shrovetide, and courtiers were badly in want of a select resort of the kind. In playing the rôle of host to his pretended guests he was, of course, sailing close to the wind, but he could reckon upon the countenance of the Queen, and, after all, his assemblies were small enough and well-ordered enough to be diplomatically ignored by the civic authorities. Publicity, however, had to be avoided. There could be no summoning of an audience after the manner of the common players, no setting up of bills or blowing of trumpets. But because of these limitations, it is probable that a practice at once sprang up which we find in existence in all kinds of theatres at a slightly later period, and which remained in vogue up to the last century: the practice of giving out the next play and acting day at the end of a performance.

To Sebastian Westcote the money in the scheme

AN   3

was doubtless the main urging, but his pretext was that of setting up a sort of rehearsal theatre where plays could be tested and histrionically mellowed for Court performance; and later on, this plea—a half-truth—was consistently made by his successors when a disposition was shown to challenge the legality of a "private house". Thus it was that, without loss of time, he set up a stage in the singing school of the Almonry House of St Paul's, the house in which he and his choristers lived. That this procedure was prompted by the Act of Common Council of December 1574, and was effected not long after its promulgation, is demonstrated by the fact that exactly twelve months later the Privy Council went to the trouble of issuing an order for the examination of some persons (probably associated with a troupe of common players) whom Westcote suspected of having lured away one of his boy-actors.[1] This order, on the face of it, testifies that the Master of Paul's had support in high places.

Though the patrons of the scheme were more select than numerous, the principle of the private house was economically sound. A nucleus of histrionic supply was already to hand gratis. It is true that Westcote had no more than ten boy-choristers at his command, scarcely sufficient—even if we

[1] H. N. Hillebrand, *The Child Actors, loc. cit.*

concede some mild doubling of parts and offices—
to provide a theatre with the necessary number of
players, supernumeraries and musicians. But research has recently revealed that it was possible then
to take duly indentured apprentices to learn acting,
the term usually being for three years;[1] and it seems
highly probable that Westcote supplemented his
ready-made supply by this means. Be that as it may,
the important thing to note is that his project had
only to be executed to meet with immediate and
well-sustained success, a success so complete as to
lead to its stabilisation. No doubt the good fortune
of the early private house was due to its double
appeal: it was almost as much concert hall as theatre.
Nearly all its distinguishing characteristics were the
outcome of the initial training given to the choirboys. They were nothing if not competent musicians,
and it is to their gifts and graces we owe the genesis
of that hardy hybrid known as musical comedy.

It is not too much to ask theatrical historians, when
dealing in future with the intricate story of the early
private playhouse, to speak by the card, since
equivocation on the point has for so long undone
them. From what has been already stated, it is
plainly to be seen that the institution was originally
known as a private house, and that the term for a

---

[1] H. N. Hillebrand, *The Child Actors*, Pt. II, p. 197.

3-2

considerable period signified a small amateur subscription theatre. It remains to unfold what slight
alterations in its scheme took place in the first
quarter of a century of its history, how the practice
of the principle came to be looked upon as the
prerogative of boy-players, and how, at a later
period, the name persisted long after the thing itself
had passed away.

In the circumstances (the supply of choirboys
being limited), there was no possibility of abundant
emulation of Westcote's venture, but such was its
success that in process of time another choirmaster
(who has enjoyed until recently the distinction of
having originated the private-theatre principle)
decided to follow his example. This was Richard
Farrant, Master of the Children of Windsor, who
was almost as much of a *persona grata* at Court as the
Master of Paul's. Having secured the lease of some
premises in the frater of the old Blackfriars priory
formerly occupied by Lord Cobham, Farrant proceeded, early in 1577, to convert a portion of the top
floor into a private theatre, arranging to use the
residue of the building for living purposes. Despite
the use to which he put the upper section of the
building, the whole remained a private house within
the meaning of the act. There he employed as players
and musicians not only the choirboys legally under

his control, but likewise, by arrangement with
William Hunnis their master, the Children of the
Chapel Royal. It has frequently been stated that his
aim in choosing a site for his theatre within the
Liberty of the Blackfriars was that he might thereby
gain immunity from the persecutions of the Common Council, but he was assured of that immunity
so long as he kept within the law, and it would
rather appear that he had elected to set up his theatre
in the Blackfriars for the convenience of his sub-
scribers, it being the fashionable residential district.
Even Westcote's "private house" itself was not far
away.

The curious thing is that although both theatres
appealed to the same (in the circumstances, a strictly
limited) public, both seem to have enjoyed for years
an equal prosperity. Later on, however, Paul's
seems to have suffered in the competition, with the
result that risks were taken. It sounds ominous to
learn that, before its collapse in 1589, admission
money had been accepted at the doors. But despite
this approximation to common theatrical methods,
neither Paul's nor Blackfriars was viewed as anything otherwise than "a private house". The public
theatres one and all had distinctive or fancy names—
such as the Curtain and the Rose; the private had
none. It is not until the close of James I's reign, when

the Phoenix arose, that the distinction was obliterated, and by that time, as I hope to show, the private theatre had lost every shred of its initial privacy.

As originally constituted, the private house contained the germs of its own dissolution. The canker was in the bud, but in that age of diffused musical culture, music proved for long an arresting antiseptic. It would be idle to pretend that the boys fought the men with their own weapons. The advent of Lyly and the vogue of euphuism put off for a time the evil day, but in the meanwhile the public theatre was becoming better and better organised, and it was not to be expected that any type of being in a virile adventurous epoch could remain satisfied with a pale passionless drama. Once Kyd and Marlowe had emerged, the pretty little house of cards was bound to topple over. Even when, at the close of the century, the old principle was nominally resuscitated—only nominally, for there was much loosening of the shackles—there was so little durability in the appeal of the boy-players that reliance had to be placed at all hazards on the adventitious aid of ribald personalities and gross caricature.

Though the first two private houses both contrived to survive their founders, both had closed their doors by 1586. Curiously enough, the one of lesser note, Paul's, was the first to fail and the first to be revived. What led to its resuscitation in 1598 it is difficult to know. It can hardly have been due to any urging from the Court, for the Queen had for some years discountenanced the boy-players, and no children's company was to appear again before her until 1601. But the revival of the Paul's Boys, short-lived as it proved, is of importance as showing that, despite the lapse of the principle, the validity of the "private house" had been thoroughly established, so thoroughly indeed that, as we shall shortly see, shelter could be taken behind its privileges as a *dernier ressort.*

Early in 1596, James Burbage, on finding that the expiring lease of the theatre in Shoreditch was unrenewable on reasonable terms, bought some premises in the old Blackfriars monastery and proceeded to convert them into an orthodox playhouse of medium size, a playhouse of the common order, having a pit, boxes and two galleries, but with this improvement that he purposed preserving the roof, so as to obviate most of the inconveniences of his old open house. He so far managed to keep his intentions to himself that it was not until some eight or nine months later that it dawned upon the aristocratic inhabitants of the precinct what he was about, and, as the setting up of a public theatre in their midst was calculated in their minds to create disorder "by reason of the great resort and gathering together of all manner of vagrant and lewd persons", they petitioned the Privy Council for relief from the menace. Just as the theatre was as good as finished, Burbage was forbidden to open it: a painful dilemma from which death mercifully released him early in 1597. But the worry was only transferred, for his two sons, Cuthbert and Richard, the one a bookseller and the other a noted actor, inherited the white elephant. After the building had lain idle on their hands for over two years, the brothers conceived the idea of converting in into a "private house" in the old technical acceptation of the term, wilfully ignoring the awkward circumstance that to any sort of private house it bore internally no slightest resemblance. And the strange thing was that, though a theatre, architecturally speaking, cannot well be reckoned otherwise than a theatre, their hare-brained scheme proved successful. From them Henry Evans, who had formerly managed the boy-players of Farrant's old house in its final period, took a lease of the building, and, by arrangement with Nathaniel Giles, then Master of the Children of the Chapel, established the children there late in 1600, without opposition. The fact that

the boys were amateurs and that boy-players had
been so long identified with the scheme of the
private house as to become part of it, formed the
only vestige of a reason for styling the new theatre
a private house. It probably also operated—aided
and abetted, no doubt, by some Court influence—
to silence discontent in the precinct.

At once all the main principles of the old private
house went by the board. Evans was somehow so
far assured of his position that he began following
public-theatre procedure, and besides issuing bills
of the play and giving the regulation three trumpet
(or cornet) blasts to summon his audience, actually
took money at the doors. To conciliate the Master
of the Revels licence fees were paid on all new plays.
No protests arose, and the boys, having established
their popularity by the production of some good
new pieces, found their position consolidated by
the receipt of a patent from King James in 1604,
giving them the style and title of the Children of the
Queen's Revels. With the granting of that distinction, the application of the term "private house" to
the second Blackfriars became wholly anomalous,
though persisting, and it is not surprising to find it
being rivalled by the term "private playhouse".[1]

[1] But no more than rivalled. Even in 1608, Dekker, to whom
the use of theatrical metaphor came as a second nature, could write

Following this, a second house of the new order—
the Whitefriars—was established under royal aus-
pices, its players being known as the Children of the
King's Revels. Evidently there was thought to be
money in the expanded scheme, since it soon became
commercialised. Adventurers, without possessing
any particular interest in the drama, invested in both
concerns, and there was ultimately much burning of
fingers. Thanks to their audacious resort to Aristo-
phanic satire, the boys became for a time serious
rivals of the common players, but disaster came to
the striplings of the Blackfriars when they went so
far as to scoff at the King. The main outcome of
the disgrace which followed was a further merging
of distinctions. In 1609, the King's Men took over
the vacated Blackfriars and used it regularly as a
winter theatre. This was innovation with a ven-
geance: never before had a company of profes-
sionals acted in a private house. Not that this was
the end of the boy-players. Children companies
rose and fell intermittently up to the days of Puritan
ascendancy and the outbreak of the Civil War. It
was then that Dame Fortune lowered her thumb.

In all this we have exemplification of the disturb-

in *Lanthorne and Candlelight* (ch. xii): "A thousand of these
comedies were acted in dumb shew, and onely in the *privat
houses*".

ing, if little recognised, fact that evolution is apt at any moment to jump the rails. We find an institution which in the beginning owed its right of existence to its complete privacy ending by becoming thoroughly public. Beyond the quality of the audience and the difference in the prices of admission, there was no particular distinction between the two classes of theatre in Caroline days. Both were equally public, and the contrast was one of the common and the select.

Apart from the interest attached to the unravelling of a mystery, this story of the rise and progress of the private playhouse is of prime historical importance, because it was from the private playhouse that the modern theatre took its origin. In it was first seen the seated pit (as contrasted with the standing yard of the open-air houses); and, for more than a couple of centuries, or until its rights were encroached upon by the destructive alien principle of stalls, the pit remained a characteristic British institution, the seat of judgment, a nursery of good taste, and the conservator of all that was sound in the traditions.

Chapter IV

SHAKESPEARE'S SUPERS

Every author, great or small, has his lapses, but the peculiarity about Shakespeare is that when he nods he generally has one eye open. One of the hallmarks of the true Shakespearian scholar, as distinguished from the sciolist, lies in his ability to single out the few inconsistencies in the poet's plays which are actual from the many which are apparent. For example, it is his prerogative to recognise that Shakespeare's most glaring anachronisms—Cleopatra's stay-lace, the Roman conspirators' hats, and kindred blemishes—are purposive, part of a scheme to make comprehensible to an audience, largely illiterate and narrowly insular, a remote tale of other days and other climes by telling it in a familiar way. This method was really in the air; it was abundantly precedented; it gave colour to the epic in the Middle Ages, and was even carried over into the art of historical painting at the Renascence.

Anachronisms apart, it is the great misfortune of Shakespeare that the vast majority of his readers, never having inflated their lungs by deep breathing in the Elizabethan atmosphere, see absurdities in him

where there is none. For the rigidly modern mind
there are traps in his plays into which even the semi-
scholarly have been known to tumble. One of the
best-baited[1] occurs in the description of the dumb
show preceding the by-play in *Hamlet*, as given in
the First Folio but in no other of the early texts.
While the Queen is grieving over the body of her
murdered husband, "the poysoner", we read, "with
some two or three Mutes comes in againe seeming to
lament with her" and "The dead body is carried
away". At first sight, seeing that all the participants
in a dumb show are necessarily dumb, the description of two of them as mutes seems a work of
supererogation, but sound reason for the use of the
term is reached once we plunge beneath the surface.
The truth is, though it has never yet been demonstrated, that in the Elizabethan theatre and for long
after the word "mute" was employed in exactly
the same sense as we employ the slang term "super".
It signified to Shakespeare and his fellows all those
who were pressed on occasion into service as scene-
fillers without being given a line to speak: a motley
lot, since it comprised not only the furniture- and
property-removers and stage hands generally, but
even the very doorkeepers. What, then, the careful

[1] See Dutton Cook's article on "Inexplicable Dumb Shews" in
Belgravia for August 1879, p. 193.

phrasing of the description just cited from the First
Folio conveys is that while all the acutal executants
of the pantomimic action were regular players, the
men who came on with the poisoner to remove the
dead body of the King were simply supers.

A wise economy ruled in the Elizabethan theatre.
Perhaps the only real difference between the mute
of those days and the super of ours is that the latter
receives some recompense for his supering. Even on
the rare occasions when the early seventeenth-
century players went outside the theatre for temporary recruits, they sought only for volunteer aid.
At the dawn of the Restoration, Tom Killigrew,
patentee of the King's playhouse (he was born in
1612), told his friend Samuel Pepys that in his
boyhood he had a habit of hanging about the
theatres, especially the Red Bull, and (leaving the
diarist to tell the rest of the story) "when the man
cried to the boys, 'Who will go and be a devil, and
he shall see the play for nothing?' then he would go
in, and be a devil upon the stage and so get to see
plays". Possibly Killigrew was the first super,
amateur or professional, to rise to theatrical emi-
nence, but stage history shows that he was certainly
not the last.

Scanty though the early evidence be in support of
my gloss on the term "mute", I have no doubt that

it will be deemed sufficing. As a stage technicality, rare old Ben, having fretted and strutted his brief and unsatisfactory hour upon the boards, was familiar with it, and he took it for granted that the select patrons of the Blackfriars were familiar with it too, otherwise he would hardly have used it metaphorically. Recall the scene in *Cynthia's Revels* where Crites describes the various types of gallants haunting the Court and contrives in so doing to indulge in some quaint, though none the less revealing, theatrical similes and tropes:

> There stands a neophyte glazing of his face,
> Pruning his clothes, perfuming of his hair,
> Against his idol enters; and repeats,
> Like an unperfect prologue at third music,
> His part of speeches, and confederate jests,
> In passion to himself. Another swears
> His scene of courtship over; bids, believe him,
> Twenty times ere they will; anon, doth seem
> As he would kiss away his hand in kindness;
>
> . . . .
>
> A fourth, he only comes in for a mute;
> Divides the act with a dumb show, and exit.

One has a certain malicious satisfaction in drawing Professor Dover Wilson's attention, and the attention of his mighty cohort of followers, to all, indeed, whether scholarly or otherwise, who unite in agreeing that, in his own time, Shakespeare's plays were acted all of a breath, to the plain import of this last line. It will be a delight to savour the ingenuity with which it will be explained away.

In May 1599, or about eighteen months before *Cynthia's Revels* fluttered the Whitehall dovecotes, Chettle and Dekker forestalled Shakespeare in providing the Admiral's Men with a Troilus and Cressida play. A curious relic of this piece now reposes in the British Museum. It is a fragment of an action-plot for the guidance of the players, and one of the items reveals that, once on coming on, Cressida was attended by "mutes".

Even then the term had long been in theatrical use. Proof of this comes to hand from a most unlikely source. In 1579, or a bare three years after the first English theatre was established, the Reverend William Wilkinson, a clergyman of the Established Church, wrote a little book controverting the tenets of that much-ridiculed long-suffering sect known as "The Family of Love", and, in the course of his fulminations, expressed himself as follows regarding "one H. N., a heretic":

As for his vayne and idle quotation they are innumerable, which as Mutes upon a stage called forth to fill vp a roome and make a shew depart not utteryng any word at all.

It is astonishing to find an Elizabethan divine

conversant enough with the stage to be able and willing to resort to the use of one of its technicalities, and the circumstance somehow recalls the old story of the picnic at which, by a horrible oversight, the corkscrew was forgotten, and, after a vigorous canvas of the company, the only person who confessed to carrying a pocket one was the curate.

Shakespeare, having materially assisted us in arriving at the applied use of the word "mute", receives abundant recompense, inasmuch as the knowledge so gained enables us to elucidate Shakespeare. More than once he uses the word in its theatrical sense. Listen to the ebbing Hamlet:

> You that look pale and tremble at this chance,
> That are but mutes or audience to this act,
> Had I but time—as this fell Sergeant, Death,
> Is strict in his arrest—O, I could tell you—
> But let it be.

About the only time on the old platform stage that the mutes found themselves personally referred to.[1]

[1] Note the interesting metaphorical use made of the term by Will Rowley in his dedication of *A Fair Quarrel* (1617): "If this great world is no more than a stage—indeed the players themselves have the least part of it, for I know few that have lands (which are a part of the world) and therefore no grounded men; but howsoever they serve for mutes, happily must wear good clothes for attendance, yet all have exits and all must be stript in the tiring house (viz. the grave) for none must carry any thing out of the stock".

In more ways than one, indeed, our new knowledge of the technical use of "mute" proves revealing. In the belated quarto of Lodowick Carlell's Caroline tragedy, *Osmond the Great Turk, or The Noble Servant*, the exhaustive list of *dramatis personae* includes a mention of "mutes", meaning those old Turkish executioners who were experts in the use of the bowstring. But there are similar lists in three of Massinger's plays, *The Duke of Milan*, *The Maid of Honour* and *The Emperor of the East*, in which the word occurs and in the first two of which it cannot be given the same interpretation. The mutes in *The Emperor of the East* were doubtless the executioners who came on near the end, but there were no executioners in the other two plays. In all three cases the mutes are last on the list, which, in *The Duke of Milan*, terminates with "2 Posts | A Beadle | Waiters | Mutes". Because of this curious, seemingly meticulous enumeration, one is compelled to conclude that the mutes were simply the silent attendants in the play, but, as silent attendants in an old play might almost be taken for granted, the puzzle is to know why they should have been listed. Since inclusions of the sort are utterly superfluous so far as the reader is concerned, the inference would be that lists of *dramatis personae* were not prepared primarily for the use of the reader, but for the service of the stage. In this way, the stagekeeper was warned that a certain number of attendants were required in the play, leaving it to him to determine the number.

The recurrence of "mutes" in a manuscript cast of characters in an early Restoration play indicates that, severe as had been the rupture in theatrical affairs occasioned by the Interregnum, it had not brought about any disuse of the old terms. This cast is of Ferdinando Parkhurst's lost comedy, *Ignoramus, or the Academical Lawyer*, as played at the Cockpit in Drury Lane and also before the Court at Whitehall, in 1662.[1] After detailing the principal characters and their representatives, the list ends with "A victualler | a fidler | Mutes".

Old stories assume new aspects once the obsolete terms in which they are partly told recover their pristine meanings. It has not hitherto been grasped how menial was the employment of Anne Oldfield when she first went on the stage, but, armed with our new knowledge, we can at last grasp the full import of Colley Cibber's authentic account of her novitiate. Writing of the old Drury Lane company in the ninth chapter of his *Apology*, Cibber says:

In the year 1699, Mrs Oldfield was first taken into

[1] For fuller details, see Leslie Hotson, *The Commonwealth and Restoration Stage*, p. 214.

the house, where she remain'd about a twelvemonth almost a Mute and unheeded, till Sir John Vanbrugh, who first recommended her, gave her the Part of Alinda in *The Pilgrim* revis'd.

It makes a world of difference to omit the indefinite article before "mute", as was not long ago done by Mr Lewis Melville in quoting the passage in his *Stage Favourites of the Eighteenth Century*. As we shall see anon, a later distinguished actress had a similar experience, put on record in a similar way.

Mute always by nature, the super remained mute also by name until the beginning of the nineteenth century.[1] Poetical satire yields some proof of this. In *The Rosciad*, that bombshell thrown into the theatrical camp in 1761, Churchill, in describing the fantastic imaginary pageant which heralds the coming of the various candidates for the histrionic throne, writes:

First, Order came—with solemn step, and slow,
In measur'd time his feet were taught to go.

[1] Goldsmith, in the course of his "Remarks on our Theatres" in the first number of *The Bee* (October 6, 1759), says: "Our little pages also with unmeaning faces, that bear up the train of a weeping princess, and our awkward lords in waiting, take off much from her distress. Mutes of every kind divide our attention, and lessen our sensibility; but here it is entirely ridiculous, as we see them seriously employed in doing nothing. If we must have dirty-shirted guards upon the theatres, they should be taught to keep their eyes fixed on the actors, and not roll them round upon the audience, as if they were ogling the boxes".

Behind from time to time, he cast his eye,
Lest This should quit his place, That step awry.
Appearances to save his only care;
So things seem right, no matter what they are.
In him his parents saw themselves renew'd,
Begotten by Sir Critic on Saint Prude.
Then came Drum, Trumpet, Hautboy, Fiddle, Flute;
Next Snuffer, Sweeper, Shifter, Soldier, Mute:
Legions of Angels all in white advance;
Furies all fire, come forward for a dance.

Two years later, Edward Thompson, in depicting a less imaginary procession in his ribald satire, *The Meretriciad*, paid his friend Churchill the sincerest form of flattery:

Next from each playhouse with the salt-box come,
A Snuffer, Sweeper, Trumpeter and Drum,
Then, solus, hops a dull Orchestran flute,
Behind him waddles a theatric Mute.

A score of years elapse, and still the old term remains understanded of the people. In Edward Topham's epilogue to Cumberland's comedy, *The Natural Son*, spoken at Drury Lane in 1784, mordant reference is made to the powers of newspaper puffery and to John Bull's folly in swallowing it:

Puff is the word: where fame is not a breath,
How many an actress puff has sav'd from death!
And Actors, for whom Mutes were full enough,
Have risen Alexanders—from a puff!

But not all sudden advancements were made in this way. In a scandalous little book published in 1782 and bearing title, *Theatrical Biography: or Memoirs of the Principal Performers of the Three Theatres Royal*, there is an account of the career of Mrs Yates, in which one reads:

It was under the name of Miss G——, or (to speak in the language of those who have a memory for ill-natured vulgarism) Moll G——, that Mrs Yates made her first proposals to the managers of Drury Lane; after a few rehearsals it was found her *person* only spoke in her favour, and merely on this account she was taken in under the double character of *dresser* and *mute*, at the inconsiderable salary of *twenty* shillings per week....

Naturally possessing the seeds of theatrical genius, her inclinations strongly supported them, and she neglected no opportunity to observe on the best performers, and turn that observation to advantage: it was a long time, however, before she was permitted to *speak*; at last an opportunity presented itself, the sudden illness of one of the actresses, where a good figure was necessary, obliged the prompter to look round the theatre for an immediate supply; Mrs Yates being the only person remarkably happy in this respect, was asked whether she would *attempt* it; her heart bounded at the question, she sat down to it with avidity, and, after a while, made herself so perfect in it, that her performance, like a talismanic power, broke the spells of her quondam silence, and she was im-

mediately called up to fill characters of more consequence, whilst her salary was proportionately increased.

The reference here to a not unusual combination
of the offices of dresser and mute serves to recall
that throughout the greater part of the eighteenth
century, theatrical managers were little disposed to
look beyond the people in their regular employ for
the provision of stage crowds. As often as not, the
masquerading scene-shifters and candle-snuffers
must have proved a motley, illusion-marring
assembly, something as weird in its way as "the
Adelphi guests" of a subsequent era. (Even that
term calls now for some interpretation.) As late
as November 1797, one finds a correspondent of
The Monthly Mirror making bitter plaint regarding
the ragged regiment pressed into service to act as the
chief mourners in the old interpolated funeral dirge
in a recent London revival of Garrick's sophistica-
tion of *Romeo and Juliet*. But it would be idle to
deduce from this that no betterment of the bad old
system had as yet taken place. When the musical
entertainment of *Arthur and Emmeline* was in rehearsal for its production at Drury Lane in November 1784, Thomas Linley the musician, who was then
in charge of affairs, engaged a number of soldiers to
act as supers. His wife, a rigid economist, was very
indignant over this extravagance, and gave vent to

her feelings in a manner amusingly recorded by her daughter:

"Oh...Tickell, I'm fretted to death. These Devils! but it's all Mr. King's fault."—"Why, what's the matter, ma'am?"—"Why, do you know they've hired a whole Regiment of Guards a'most for Arthur, and for what? as I said—for you know, there's plenty of common men about the house; that always comes on for sailors and why should they not make as good soldiers?"—"Why, because, forsooth, they can't march in time, ma'am."—"But my husband is such a fool."[1]

Linley's innovation marks a transitional period, though it was long before mercenary troops wholly ousted the old volunteers. That a change, however, was slowly taking place can be satisfactorily determined. Extra hands are supernumeraries, and to arrive at the time when that term first began to be employed in theatrical circles would certainly admit of a conclusion. We find Malone using it in his *Shakespeare* in 1790, when he inaccurately describes the old term "Hirelings" as "men hired occasionally by the night: in modern language, *supernumeraries*". Despite its sesquipedalianism, it had come to stay, but it had to fight for its foothold. Even Cobbett, when writing in 1806 of the gaudy triumphal car in

[1] R. Crompton Rhodes, *Harlequin Sheridan*, p. 102.

which Sheridan and Hood rode after the famous Westminster election, proved a reactionary:

The car which had been constructed by the people of Drury Lane, was surrounded by beadles, constables, police-officers, and police-magistrates, and as even their own venal prints inform us, by the numerous officers of the Thames police. "The People", of whom they talk as *huzzaers*, consisted of the play-actors, scene-shifters, candle-snuffers, and mutes of the Theatre, aided by a pretty numerous bevy of those unfortunate females who are in some sort inmates of that mansion, so that altogether the procession bore a very strong resemblance to that of *Blue Beard*.[1]

It is an interesting question how long it was before "supernumeraries" became contracted in theatrical and popular parlance into the now familiar "supers". Seemingly the truncation did not take place for a very many years. There is still extant a contract between Elliston, the famous manager of old Drury, and George Smith the actor, entered into in October 1822, in which details are given of the regulation charge for benefits, exclusive of the charge for "new dresses, printing, advertising, supernumeraries, etc." Dickens, who was familiar with the theatre of his time, uses the full term twice—once in *Sketches by Boz* (1836) and once in *Pictures from Italy* (1844)— but is innocent of its abbreviation. Not until the

[1] R. Crompton Rhodes, *op. cit.* p. 216.

early fifties do we find "super" creeping into print. Thirty years later, its vogue became momentarily threatened by a change which came over the spirit of the theatrical dream. With Henry Irving to the fore, the stage suddenly sloughed its old skin and came to be looked upon as a quite genteel profession. "We put our sons to it", said Lord Houghton on an historic occasion. And so it happened that even the long-despised supers came to be treated with some respect. They were given brevet rank, and honoured with the denomination of "extra ladies and gentle-men"—generally shortened, however, to "extras". But, you may break, you may shatter the vase as you will, yet the epithet "supers" clings to them still.

Chapter V

THE DUMB SHOW IN *HAMLET*

It is difficult to reconcile the maturer Shakespeare's universally conceded mastery of stagecraft with the gross blunder in tactics made by heralding *The Murder of Gonzago* with a forestalling dumb show. To say that it is superfluous is not to say all, for its realistic advancement of the scheme of the by-play is excellently calculated to defeat the primary purpose by putting the bloat King on his guard against the trap which has been laid for him. Nor will it suffice to plead that, grave blemish as it is, it must be pardoned on the score of conventionality. Though there was precedent for the device, there was none for its particular usage. To ponder over these valid objections is to have one's curiosity aroused concerning the wherefore of its origin, a fascinating problem which nobody has ever attempted to solve. Nevertheless, there is little room to doubt that in its abnormality lies its secret. The ensuing investigation of the crux is designed to show the high probability that lost stage history remains embedded in the mystery, that the offending dumb show, inoffensive and necessary at the period of its origin, owed the insensate prolongation of its existence, after the purpose which created it had been served, to the arbitrary and time-serving attitude of Shakespeare's fellows.

Unexampled as is the dumb show in some respects, it is not by dint of its initiatory office that it possesses any particular distinctiveness. About half a dozen instances are known in the popular drama of Shakespeare's day (one, at least,—in *Locrine*—preceding *Hamlet*) in which pantomimic action opened the play. But in all these cases the dumb show was of a different nature from the dumb show in *The Murder of Gonzago* and followed a different routine. Some are obscurely symbolic, as in *Locrine*; some are simply introductory, as in *The Four Prentices of London*; and some convey the antecedents of the plot, as in *The Divil's Charter*. Generally speaking, dumb shows were of an emblematic order, prefiguring somewhat vaguely the nature of the action which was to follow, pictorial charades, as John Addington Symonds once neatly styles them, "inexplicable" in the ill-comprehended Shakespearian sense, inasmuch as their meaning was not to be grasped without the aid of an interpreter. Hence we find that in all these preluding examples, save in the noteworthy exception in *Hamlet*, either the Prologue introduced and expounded the dumb show, as in *The Weakest*

Goes to the Wall and *The Whore of Babylon,* or the task of exposition, as in *The Four Prentices of London,* fell to a special presenter. The fact is not without significance that Shakespeare for the most part followed common routine in the rustic interlude in *A Midsummer Night's Dream,* indulging, however, in some exaggeration for burlesque purposes, especially in making the presenter describe the characters in the dumb show as if they were so many waxwork figures.

What we require, then, first to grasp is that, *Hamlet* apart, such a thing as an unexpounded initiatory dumb show is unknown in Elizabethan drama. That lack is surely a sign-post pointing to the rugged road leading to a solution. Next, we have to ask ourselves why Shakespeare's Prologue (having nothing particular to say, and saying it in the briefest possible manner) should have delayed coming on until the dumb show had departed, instead of appearing at the very beginning. Also, why Hamlet (in the received text of to-day, as based on the Second Quarto), though familiar with the play, should fancy that the Prologue is going to interpret the dumb show when he is going to do nothing of the kind. No purpose is served in prevaricating with Ophelia or deceiving the real audience.

The truth is that all the evidence, as we have it, favours the supposition—never yet, I think, advanced by anyone—that Shakespeare was in no wise responsible for the dumb show. Lewis Theobald gave it as his opinion that the description of the show should be altered so as to make it in keeping with the by-play, i.e. by converting the King and Queen into a Duke and Duchess with regal coronets. Here he drew attention to a curious incongruity, of itself significant enough to all who are capable of reading between the lines. It is surely obvious that, if the dumb show and the play had been devised and written by the one hand at the one time, the principals in both would have been made to correspond. Accordingly, we are forced to conclude that Shakespeare wrote *The Murder of Gonzago* for performance without any dumb show, and is not to be held responsible for its subsequent disfigurement.

In all probability, the circumstances were much as the following. In 1594, the Lord Chamberlain's men purchased the crude, well-worn old Hamlet play, and then, or later, placed it in Shakespeare's hands for revision. The story of the stage treatment of the old Danish saga in the latter half of the sixteenth century proves to be the exact reverse of the transmutation undergone by Sir John Cutler's famous stockings, which, it will be recalled, though

silk in the beginning, were so frequently darned that
they eventually became worsted. What is remarkable, after making all due allowance for Shakespeare's overwhelming genius, is that all trace of the
identity of the author of the initial Hamlet play
should have disappeared. Meres's silence on the
point in 1598 admits of the inference that, whether
or not he had in any wise revised the old text,
Shakespeare had not as yet put his seal on the subject.

Though the truth about the matter has been
hitherto obscured, there is good reason to believe
that in the primary treatment of the theme, the
dumb show, precisely in the form in which it has
come down to us, constituted the whole of the by-
play, or, in other words, that the crisis was reached
before the play proper began. (Once established,
this would negative the supposition that the concocter of the spurious *Hamlet* Quarto drew partly on
the older play and partly on Shakespeare for the text
of his by-play.) Only in this way can one account
for the unprecedented presentation of the argument
in the dumb show: unprecedented, that is, in any
play where the dumb show was a mere preliminary.
Thoroughly to catch the conscience of the King,
the guilty lovers were made of regal rank, and the
circumstances compelled the two (for identification
purposes) to wear their crowns even in the privacy

of their orchard. The King in his actually lies down on a flowery bank to take a rest. It may be safely assumed that a brief Prologue preceded the dumb show, and that a presenter came on afterwards to put the action of the pantomime into words. So tellingly was this done, that the remorse-bitten Claudius, unable to face a third and fuller exposition of his crime, fled incontinently before the play began.

It may be that the effect came tardily off, or it may be that there was a desire to give the scene some fillip of novelty, but, whatever the reason, Shakespeare apparently wrote the play on the prescribed lines, about a Duke and a Duchess, ignoring the old dumb show, which had then become superfluous. So far all is pretty plain sailing, but the rest is difficult. Since, however, a theory has to be propounded, might it not have been that, when the revision was put in rehearsal, the routine-ridden players, fearing that the groundlings would protest vigorously against the excision of the familiar dumb show, insisted, despite Shakespeare's remonstrances about the absurdity of the thing, upon its preservation? (It has always been the same story. Modern new plays have been ruined, time and again, in the same senseless way.) To square the by-play with the old dumb show, the speech headings specifying the Duke and Duchess were altered in the prompt-book to the King and Queen, though the text itself still referred to the old ducal rank of the two.

It would be idle to attempt to argue away the persistence of the original dumb show. True enough, certain passages omitted in the old play in the acting were often marked linearly in the left-hand margin of the prompt-book, without cancellation, with the result that when the book was sent to the printer, the omitted passages often found their way into print. But this cannot have happened in this particular case. Not only has the dumb show (with slight variance in the wording but none in the details) a place in the First and Second Quartos and the Folio, but it must be borne in mind that the spurious Quarto was printed from the pirated prompt-book of a country company, a book not likely to contain anything superfluous. We may take it that, yielding reluctantly to the arbitrary eleventh-hour decision of his fellows, Shakespeare wrote in a few connecting links between the dumb show and the play, an unfortunate interpolation which had the defect of assigning the Prologue (correctly placed before) to an improper position. This blemish, ugly as it appears now, did not, however, matter much: the main misfortune of the added colloquy between Hamlet and Ophelia was that it aroused expectations which were not to be

AN   5

gratified: a result so risky that further tinkering with the text at this juncture became necessary. In this connexion, it must be borne in mind that in the received *Hamlet* text of to-day, the play-scene is printed almost wholly from the Second Quarto, a version of the play made in 1600,[1] and that in the Folio the dialogue, coming immediately after the dumb show, runs somewhat differently, and has a different significance. No one can say for certain when the Folio version was made, but it is assuredly a later text and belongs to the Jacobean period. In the Second Quarto, but not in the Folio, it is to be noted that the Prologue makes his entry just as Ophelia says: "Belike this show imports the argument of the play". To that impression Hamlet accedes, though, being conversant with the play, he ought surely to have known better; his reply puts the audience on a wrong scent through conveying the idea that the fellow who has just come on is a presenter. (The Hamlet of the spurious First Quarto is even more deceiving, for, in response to Ophelia's "What means this, my lord?" he actually says: "you shall hear anone; this fellow will tell all".)

---

[1] See my paper on "The date of Shakespeare's *Hamlet*" in *Shakespeare's Workshop*. After the evidence here advanced, it is surprising that some scholars should still retain the old belief and continue to assign the play to 1601. See, for example, Dr G. B. Harrison's pleasant book on *Shakespeare at Work*.

But in the Folio this fault is amended. There, in response to Ophelia's surmise, Hamlet says: "we shall know by these Fellowes: the Players cannot keepe counsell, they'l tell all", evidently meaning: "have patience: the play will answer the question". Moreover, it is not until after Ophelia has persisted with "Will they tell us what this show meant?", and Hamlet has made smutty reply, that the Prologue enters.

When the text had reached this stage, it would have been an easy matter to remove all the blemishes from the scene by eliminating all the action and dialogue from Hamlet's speech ending with "the hobby horse is forgot" unto the entrance of the Prologue. This was eventually done, and, once done, done for good;[1] but it is a nice question when the players made atonement for the aspersion that Shakespeare's fellows had (unwittingly) cast upon his judgment. A little surmise on the point is perchance allowable. We know that at the Restoration a monopoly of certain of Shakespeare's plays was given to Davenant's company, among them *Hamlet*, notable as the first to be acted with scenery. In 1676, a quarto of the tragedy giving an inde-

[1] In the early eighteenth-century reprints of *Hamlet* the dumb show is omitted and the text manipulated accordingly, but in a very clumsy manner.

pendent text was printed, bearing the equivocal intimation, "as it is now Acted at his Highness the Duke of York's Theatre". Wherein the equivocation lay is demonstrated in the following extract from the "Address to the Reader":

This play being too long to be conveniently Acted, such Places as might be the least prejudicial to the Plot or sense, are left out upon the Stage; but that we may no way wrong the incomparable Author are here inserted according to the Original Copy with this Mark, "

Almost a fifth of the text was so marked, and, among the omissions, one finds the dumb show.[1] There was probably as much time at the disposal of the players in the Caroline theatre as there was in the Restoration theatre, since there were musical intermissions in both, and the introduction of scenery caused practically no delay, seeing that it consisted of no more than flats and wings and could be readily shifted in full sight of the audience. Consequently, if cuts were essential later, they were also essential earlier. It may be that a considerable number of the omissions indicated in the Restoration quarto were regularly made at least as early as Caroline days, and

---

[1] For fuller details, see Hazelton Spencer's *Shakespeare Improved*, pp. 174–84. Also the same writer's article on "Seventeenth-century cuts in Hamlet's soliloquies" in *The Review of English Studies* for July 1933.

that it was then the old dumb show received its quietus. We know from the *Roscius Anglicanus* of John Downes the prompter that Davenant taught Betterton to play Hamlet after the manner of Taylor, a testimony to Davenant's early familiarity with the acting version of the play. And for aught we know to the contrary, the Caroline prompt-book may have survived.

Scholarship may be confidently challenged to propound an alternative theory accounting for the existence of the offending dumb show and its contiguous peculiarities. No doubt that will be attempted: never was there a time when so much ingenuity was expended (largely to no purpose) in the solving of Shakespearian problems. But, in the circumstances, there is one thing, with all its fine resources, scholarship cannot do. It is wholly impotent to redeem Shakespeare's reputation from the stigma unjustifiably put upon it. The interloping dumb show must, perforce, remain embedded in the text until the "crack o' doom".

Chapter VI

BEARERS FOR THE DEAD

Among the divers conventions to which the peculiar construction and limitations of the Elizabethan theatre gave rise is one that has received no consideration, the provision of bearers for the dead. With an open stage projecting half across the auditorium and, owing to the absence of a front curtain, always remaining in sight, it was essential that the dead bodies which in those days of high tragedy often littered the boards should be removed before the close of the scene. At first sight, that does not appear to be a matter of much difficulty or demanding any particular forethought. The liveried stage hands were accustomed to the carrying on and off of tables and stools in the midst of the action, and one would be inclined to believe that it was left to them to remove the dead. Nothing could be wider of the mark. The dead were not considered as so much lumber: it is idle to suppose that even in Shakespeare's day there was no respect for the illusion of the scene. To obviate its marring, it was the business of the dramatist to arrange fittingly and

opportunely for the removal of the bodies either by
some of the characters in the play or their immediate
attendants. Discrimination had to be exercised in
accordance with the rank and attributes of the
person to be carried off. Generally speaking,
monarchs, nobles and great military commanders
were borne away processionally on the shoulders of
four bearers in a dead march, with a trailing of pikes
and firing of ordnance. (Death having paid off old
scores, Aufidius in *Coriolanus* is not too proud to act
as a bearer.) But with miscreants it was different.
Rank or no rank, so far from being treated with
any ceremony, their bodies were dragged out
ignominiously by the heels. This distinction is well
marked at the close of *Titus Andronicus* and *Cupid's
Revenge*. In the latter, Ismenas says:

Agenor, goe and let the Trumpets sound
Some mournefull thing, whilst we convey the body
Of this unhappy Prince into the Court,
And of that vertuous Virgin [Urania] to a grave:
But dragge her [Bacha] to a ditch, where let her lye
Accurst, whilst one man has a memory.

It was not, however, all plain sailing. Difficulties
frequently arose. Sometimes the story of the play
demanded that a death should occur in the middle of
an act in such circumstances that the removal of the
body was impossible. It is true that the Elizabethan

dramatist was not called upon for the exercise of his ingenuity in all cases of the kind, since the construction of his stage afforded a ready means of solving a good many of the problems. In the tiring house at the back was a central curtained room in which murders could be readily perpetrated, and the horrible sight as readily obscured from view. By placing Desdemona's bed on this inner stage in the last act of *Othello*, Shakespeare avoided the absurdity of bringing on bearers at the end to remove the Moor and his slaughtered lady from their own home. Remark that not only is Desdemona smothered in the bed, but the dying Emilia drags herself to its side, and Othello himself falls across it at the close. So, too, all necessity for the bearing out of the dead in the last act of *Romeo and Juliet* was precluded by the forethought of the dramatist. The three unfortunate lovers were already in a graveyard, and that sufficed: in death they were not divided. Such was the impression given to the Elizabethan audience, but there have been commentators who, forgetting that circumstances alter cases, have taken a different reading. It has been argued that the hard and fast necessity to bear off the bodies at the end determined the particular conclusion of the play.[1] On more than one count this is a fallacy. The play followed the

[1] Eric Blom, *The Limitations of Music*, p. 62.

common principle of "all on at the end". Shake-speare so carefully followed that principle that he actually put a short speech into Montague's mouth explaining why his wife and Benvolio were not present. Doubtless the players of the two were doubling other parts. Moreover, Shakespeare gives an early hint that on this occasion bearers were not to be used. Paris, when mortally wounded, begs to be placed in Juliet's tomb, and Romeo, on dis-covering his identity, complies.

But there were many intermediate death scenes where the curtained room could not be availed of nor bearers brought in, and the difficulty was to accomplish the removal of the bodies without transcending probability. Here, as elsewhere, Shake-speare evinced his superior stagecraft. Perhaps the best example of how not to do it is afforded us in the old play of *Mucedorus*, in one of whose early scenes the Clown is simply brought on that he may stumble over the dead body of the Wild Man and carry it off without a word of surprise or explanation. Contrast the brilliant manner in which Shakespeare gets rid of Hotspur's corpse in 1 *Henry IV*. Equally neat is his solution of the problem presented in the middle of the fourth act of *King Lear*, where the Steward, on receiving his death-blow, begs for a clean burial, precisely the sort of thing that, without the entreaty,

he would hardly have received at his slayer's hands.
Yet Edgar finally drags out the body with the
avowed intention of fulfilling the request. It cannot
be but that the puzzle set by the necessity for these
removals often exercised the great poet's mind.
None knew better than he that at such junctures
absurdity was always lurking round the corner; and
his reflections on the point are to be surmised from
the grim humour of Theseus's comment on the
interlude, "Moonshine and Lion are left to burie the
dead".

Credit where credit is due. Other dramatists
beside Shakespeare showed ingenuity when confronted with similar difficulties. There is a scene in
the last act of Smith's *The Hector of Germany*—a play
acted at the Red Bull in or about 1615—in which
Young Fitzwaters contrives by a stratagem, unaided
and alone, to bring about the death of three scoun-
drels, and, in order that no trace of them should be
found, flings their bodies and their weapons into the
river. With existing ideas of the ill-equipment of
the old platform stage that sounds as if it would
have required some doing, but the thing was
really simple. When realisation was impossible,
the Elizabethan players relied on suggestion.
A sloping property moss bank, placed in the entrance to the inner stage, stood for the river bank,

and over it Young Fitzwaters rolled the three bodies.

Occasionally, in reading old plays, one comes across a stray situation in which, owing to the absence of a necessary stage direction, it is impossible to divine how the bodies littering the rush-strewn boards were cleared away. Perhaps what is the most remarkable example is to be found in Shirley's late Caroline tragedy, *The Cardinal*. At the end of the fourth act of this fine play a duel occurs in which the seconds also fight, none save the four being present. Three are killed in the encounter. After Colombo's death, Hernando, the sole survivor, mutters, "I must not stay to bury him", and hurries away. Here the act ends, and one is forced to ask oneself what became of the dead bodies. A duel of four cannot have taken place otherwise than on the open stage, and it is hardly conceivable that each contestant on receiving his quietus took care to fall back through the rear-stage curtains. Yet what other solution is admittable?

There is a mystery of the sort in *Macbeth*, not of Shakespeare's making, but created by the remorseless cutting down of what, even in its ruins, is a great masterpiece. In act v, sc. 7, Macbeth encounters young Seyward when the two are alone, kills him and departs. Attracted by the noise, Macduff comes on, sees nothing of the dead body and goes his way. Next Malcolm and old Seyward arrive and prove equally short-sighted. In the next scene, we find Ross telling old Seyward that his son has paid a soldier's debt, and has been carried off the field. One is forced to ask by whom and when.

With the Civil War came the end of a chapter but not of the story. Once Stuart rule was resumed, the distressed players, after years of suppression, joyously took up acting again in the few old play-houses puritanical fury had left them, contented in being able to fall back on their well-worn repertory of old plays and to stage them in the old simple manner. This, however, was no more than a marking of time. Changes were looming on the horizon. Before long the normal attractions of the theatre were given added magnetism by the advent of the woman-player. Next, a special type of house came to be built to admit of the regular use of movable scenery. It was the inauguration of a new era, yet though modernity had begun, the changes in theatrical routine were by no means as drastic as might have been expected. Rich new wine came from the press but it was proffered in old bottles. Stage scenery, though calling for the observance of its own laws, was forced by the unreflecting players to conform with the methods of the dead-and-gone platform stage. Consequently, dramaturgy, in face of the fact that the conditions postulated a revolutionary technique, pursued a reactionary policy. Little wonder that one or two old stage conventions which should have been allowed to die a natural death actually gained renewed vitality. Though it is difficult at first sight to see the association, the persistence of the old principle of bearers for the dead was wholly owing to the imperfect stage lighting of the time. This defect was remarked by Flecknoe, who, in his *Short Discourse of the English Stage*, written in 1664, acknowledged that the French and Italians were our masters in the matter of stage spectacle, "we especially not knowing yet how to place our lights for the more advantage and illuminating the scenes".

What we require to bear in mind is that while the modern theatre dates from the Restoration, the Restoration theatre was not of the present peepshow order. It introduced the proscenium arch and the front curtain, but in such a way that only a casual use could be made of their services. There was as much stage space in front of the proscenium as behind it. In the days before the Civil War, the players had been accustomed to acting for the most part on an open platform jutting out half-way into the auditorium, and, in keeping with this principle, the Restoration theatre was provided with a capacious apron in front of the proscenium, on either side of which were permanent entering doors. Over the apron hung the majority of the chandeliers, and, to get into the focus, the player had to come well to the front. Action, of course, was not always confined there, but, generally speaking, the scenery was no more than a dim and distant background. It was impossible to avail of the friendly shelter of the curtain at the end of an act when the action had taken place in front of it, one reason, perhaps, why the curtain, once it was raised, usually remained up until the end of the play—a practice followed until well into the eighteenth century.

Sustained ridicule can annihilate most mundane follies, but the principle of bearers for the dead proved impervious to the shafts of the satirist and pursued its course oblivious of the ribald laughter of "the gods". The caution which the dramatist had to exercise under its ruling as to the number of people he could safely kill off at a time is amusingly glanced at by Buckingham in *The Rehearsal*. After the scene in which a battle is fought between (hobby) horse and foot, and Drawcansir rushes in and exterminates the lot, Smith asks Bayes, "How shall all these dead men go off?—for I see none alive to help 'em"; and Bayes replies, "Go off, why, as they came on; upon their legs: how should they go off? Why do you think the people here don't know they are not dead?"

Though laughter and ridicule failed to kill the practice, they had the salutary effect of giving the sensitive dramatist pause. In the epistle dedicatory to his version of *King Lear*, as published in 1681, Nahum Tate apologises for his alteration of Shakespeare's ending by saying:

This Method necessarily threw me on making the Tale conclude in a Success to the innocent distressed Persons: Otherwise I must have incumbred the Stage with dead Bodies, which Conduct makes many Tragedies conclude with unseasonable jests.

Tate was doubtless referring here to the flippant comments of the wits in the pit, but the unseasonable jests with which tragedies often concluded were not always of the audience's making. Nothing if not cynical, the Restoration dramatist had the demoralising habit of finishing up his labours by poking fun at the illusion he had been striving to create. Liberties were taken with the polished audience of Dryden's day that would not have been tolerated by the unsophisticated Elizabethan public. There was absolutely no precedent for the profound ill-taste of the Restoration epilogue whose double offence lay first in deriding the pathos and the moral of the play, and next in pandering to the filthy minded. It was an evil communication that for long corrupted good judgment. An ugly convention was thus established which, despite the protests of *The Spectator* and a few self-respecting dramatists, held its ground for well nigh a century. In vain did Thomson deplore the practice when, in his epilogue to *Tancred and Sigismunda*, he made the Tragic Muse say:

> Hence with your flippant epilogue, that tries
> To wipe the virtuous tear from British eyes;
> That dares my moral, tragic scene profane,
> With strains at best unsuiting light and vain.

Some years previously Budgell had attempted to defend this baneful practice by maintaining that the epilogue was something wholly separate from the play, a sort of concluding farce, but he overlooked the fact that it was commonly spoken by an actress in character, in the particular character she had sustained in the play, an association which negatived his argument. The worst offence of the sort had been committed early in his career by no less a person than Dryden. This was at the close of *Tyrannic Love, or The Royal Martyr*, when that rhyming, ranting tragedy was produced at the Theatre Royal in 1669. Valeria, the tyrant's daughter, is lying stiff and stark on the stage after having stabbed herself, and the bearers approach to bear her out. No sooner are

hands laid upon her than the character disappears
and the actress who played the part takes its place.
It is Nell Gwyn, not Valeria, who bounces up
indignantly and cries:

> Hold! are you mad? you damn'd confounded dog!
> I am to rise and speak the epilogue.
> I come, kind gentlemen, strange news to tell ye:
> I am the ghost of poor departed Nelly,

with a good deal more in the same light vein. Most
assuredly, to take such a liberty with an audience
was "beyond the purpose of playing", and, if it
failed to make the judicious grieve, it must have been
that sticklers for propriety had deserted the theatre.
To the credit of old playgoers, however, it must be
said that, although there were a good many subsequent cases where the exponent of a character
killed in the play spoke the epilogue in character, up
to the production of Cumberland's *The Battle of
Hastings* in 1778, there is only one possible instance
where Dryden's exhibition of bad taste could have
been paralleled. In Lee's *Alcibiades*, in 1675, Mrs
Mary Lee, as the dead Queen, is made to ask:

> Now, who says Poets don't in blood delight?
> . . . .
> Ours made such havock, that the silly rogue
> Was forc'd to make me rise for th'epilogue.

The persistent need for the removal of bodies in

full sight of the audience gave rise from time to time to a good many ludicrous happenings. Miss Bellamy tells a quaint story in her *Apology* of Mrs Hamilton, a popular mid-eighteenth-century actress whose misfortune at the height of her career was to be encumbered with fat. Once when she had duly passed away in the orthodox way as Arpasia in *Tamerlane*, the bearers found great difficulty in lifting the chair in which the ample remains reposed. Irritated beyond endurance by the loud guffaws of some foplings in the pit, she ordered the men to cease their struggles, and, after rising and making a courtesy to the house, walked calmly off, as if the illusion of the scene were a matter of no particular consequence.

It is curious, even significant, that anybody should have deemed it necessary in the penultimate decade of the century to give instructions to budding dramatists how to preclude the necessity of bringing on the old bearers. Writing in *The Gentleman's Magazine* in May 1789, "Dramaticus" points out the advisability of confining slaughter to the finale or last act of the play, since the fall of the curtain would satisfactorily remove the dead from sight, and prevent a sudden descent from the sublime to the ridiculous. "It cannot be denied", he writes, "that the carrying off stiffened and counterfeit bodies is so laughable an artifice it is sure to excite a risibility and turn the whole into a tragi-comic farce."

The truth is that, owing to the mysterious workings of inertia, old stage conventions had the provoking faculty of long outliving their pristine efficacy. But this particular one, after lasting from Shakespeare's day to Sheridan's, was now in the throes of dissolution.

Chapter VII

BELLS IN THE ELIZABETHAN DRAMA

It can be readily understood why the ringing of bells should have formed so prominent a feature in early theatrical representation. In all modern drama devoid of background—and the fact applies as much to the broadcast drama of to-day as to the drama of the Elizabethan era—the need has been found to procure atmosphere suggestively, by careful attention to the illusion of sounds. Granted an imaginative audience, and time and place can be as neatly conjured up in this way as by resorting to painted scenery and the juggling of lights.

There can be little doubt that one of the main uses of the flag-surmounted tower in the view of the old Globe given in Visscher's pictorial map of London was to house the large bell which had such a variety of offices that it must have proved the most useful of theatrical accessories. This was the bell which, after the firing of ordnance, gave the signal for the wholesale slaughter of the Huguenots in Marlowe's *The Massacre of Paris*; the bell, which, to Barabbas's great delight, tolled the knell of the poisoned nuns in his *Jew of Malta*; and it was likewise the bell which gave the alarm in *Macbeth* and *Othello*. In a few plays it was given a local habitation and a name, and deftly used to indicate the hour. In Haughton's *Englishmen for My Money* it had a double duty of this order. First, it represented the Exchange Bell, and by its ringing conveyed that it was noon and dinner-time; later on it stood for Bow-bell, and, in accord with nightly custom, reminded Pisaro that it was nine o'clock.[1] Doubtless the loud bell that rang out the dinner hour in *The Roaring Girl* was also intended to represent the Exchange Bell. Again, there is much rejoicing in the last act of Dekker's sweet-tasting comedy, *The Shoemaker's Holiday*, when the pancake-bell makes itself heard; and no wonder, seeing that Simon Eyre, the new Lord Mayor, had conveyed to one and all how he had arranged "that upon every Shrove Tuesday, at the sound of the pancake bell, my fine dapper Assyrians shall clap up their shop-windows and away".

Since the tower bell, when rung, had to be rung opportunely, there is good reason to believe that the rope by which it was worked descended through the tiring house to stage level. There were even occasions

---

[1] Stow tells us that "in the year 1469 it was ordained by a Common Council that the Bow bell should be nightly rung at nine of the clock".

when it could be rung from the stage itself. The most
notable example occurs in the fourth act of Heywood's striking Red Bull play, *The Golden Age*.
Danae has been confined in a gloomy tower by the
sea, and is permitted no visitor save the King. A
strict look-out is kept, and at the approach of anyone "the 'larum bell rings". This was doubtless the
same bell as was used for another purpose later in the
act. Jupiter, accompanied by a clown, comes on in
the disguise of a pedlar, and approaches the castle
gates. To gain access, he bids his companion ring the
bell, and the clown replies, "Nay, do you take the
rope in hand for luck's sake". Then, Jupiter rings
the bell.

It is interesting to note that in old stage parlance
"clock" and "bell" were synonymous terms. The
reason of this was that house clocks in Elizabethan
days were practically unknown, and that consequently the clock which was heard striking in the
theatre was always a sonorous public clock, and had
to be represented by the tower bell. The resulting
synonymy accounts for Shakespeare's peculiar use
of the word bell. In *King John*, III, 3, the King says,
while speaking to Hubert:

> ...if the midnight bell
> Did, with his iron tongue and brazen mouth,
> Sound one into the drowsy race of night.

Steevens, miscomprehending the allusion here, proposed at first to amend the passage by reading "sound on", but, on second thoughts, recanted. Perhaps he recalled Bernardo's account of the first appearance of the ghost in the opening scene of *Hamlet*:

> Last night of all,
> When yond same star that's westward from the pole
> Had made his course to illume that part of heaven
> Where now it burns, Marcellus and myself,
> The bell then beating one—

To prevent confusion between the clock and the bell (most likely to occur when the clock struck the larger hours), it was usual when striking took place for someone to count the hours. One readily recalls how Iachimo does so in the scene in Imogen's chamber, but the most curious instance in Elizabethan drama is to be found in the fourth act of *The Atheist's Tragedie*. "Twelve", ejaculates Charlemont, after listening to the striking of the hour; and Borachio, who is dogging his footsteps with murderous intent, adds, in a grimly humorous aside, "'Tis a good hour; 'twill strike one anon".

Here we arrive by natural transition at a knotty problem presented in the second act of *Macbeth*. We are not told how it was arranged that the time of Duncan's murder should be left to the determination and caprice of Lady Macbeth. All we can divine on that score comes from Macbeth's seemingly innocent instruction:

> Go bid thy mistress, when my drink is ready,
> She strike upon the bell.

Then, some twenty-nine lines later, towards the end of Macbeth's soliloquy, "a bell rings", and he closes his ruminations with

> ...the bell invites me.
> Hear it not, Duncan, for it is a knell
> That summons thee to Heaven, or to hell.

One would be glad to be able to relieve our supreme poet of the responsibility of having written such horrible clap-trap. Something is evidently wrong somewhere. Seymour, a century-old commentator whom Furness has resurrected, saw this:

> Macbeth wanted no such mechanical signal as a bell for the performance of the murder; the bell, which afterwards strikes, is the clock, which, accidentally, and with much more solemnity, reminds him it is time to dispatch.

Yes, but if it was the clock, and not the table-bell that gave the warning, why trouble to send the message to Lady Macbeth? The truth is that the existence of this crux is one more indication that the text of the play has come down to us in a revised and abbreviated state. But as it happens, a clue remains to show what was the original understanding between husband and wife as to the time for committing the murder. The hour fixed was two o'clock. Proof of this is to hand in the sleep-walking scene, where Lady Macbeth says, "One: Two: Why then 'tis time to do't". So far, so good: the only real puzzle is to determine why, on second thoughts, the tinkling of a table-bell should have been substituted for the more impressive striking of the clock.

No Elizabethan scholar with a well-stored mind can ponder for long over the use of the clock in our early drama without recalling several highly emotional scenes. Few but will have visions of that stirring climax in Marlowe's masterpiece wherein Faustus's agony becomes intensified as he counts the short time remaining to him. There is a modern recurrence of this gripping dramatic effect in *The Hour Glass* of Mr W. B. Yeats, but in this play, as I quite well remember from seeing its performance years ago at the Abbey Theatre, the tensity is less severe, owing to the gradation being procured by silent means. The mere striking of the hours and half-hours made all the difference. How a sequence of sound illusions can at once create atmosphere and accentuate a tragic situation is perhaps best illustrated by that powerful scene in the last act of *The Changeling*, where Beatrice in her anxiety counts the strokes of the clock and afterwards listens with horrible relief to the ringing of the alarm bell and the discharge of the musket.

Useful as was the old tower bell in a variety of ways, there were many bell effects for which it could not answer. Take, for example, that scene in the first act of Brome's Blackfriars play, *The Queen's Exchange*, which opens with confused sounds of shouting, mingled with strains of music and the pealing of bells, all signs and tokens of the rejoicing over the King's nuptials. Still more eloquent of the technical expertness attained in the Caroline theatre is that unique scene in the fourth act of Fletcher and Shirley's comedy, *The Night Walker, or The Little Thief*, where the action takes place in front of a church. Inside, a bell-ringing competition is going on over a wager, and, ever and anon, the bells keep pealing out. Though we cannot say for certain how these effects were procured, there is a sufficiency of evidence to warrant us in making a reasonable guess. In an inventory of the properties belonging to the Admiral's Men made by Philip Henslowe in 1598 at a time when they were acting at the Rose, one of the items reads: "Item, ij stepells, and j chyme of belles, and j beacon". The fact that this bell-pealing contrivance was a movable affair and not a permanent theatrical fixture indicates that it was, most likely, taken with them by the players when they went on tour, and was made by them to answer for all the kinds of bells required in the course of their rural performances. Without its aid they would often have been nonplussed. As to its nature, one can make a pretty good guess: apparently it was a very old device. In the *Theorica Musice* of Gafurius, printed at Milan in 1492 and notable as the earliest known treatise on music, there is a page of illustrations in four compartments dealing with the putative inventions of Pythagoras. In the same section in which a man is shown playing on the musical glasses, another man is to be seen doing the work of a whole set of bell-ringers. Six large bells of varying sizes are suspended close together on an iron rod at a height of about six feet from the ground, and on them the man is playing by means of long metal bars held in either hand.[1] This arrangement, if placed on a strong movable stand fashioned after the manner of a towel rail, would certainly have answered the Elizabethan players for bell-pealing both in town and country. One highly popular old play, *The Merry Devil of Edmonton*, positively demands some such contrivance. In the induction

[1] Cf. George Kinsky, *A History of Music in Pictures*, p. 46, miniatures of the thirteenth century. In one of these a musician is shown playing seven bells hanging on a stand.

we see Peter Fabel, the magician, asleep on his bed
at midnight, and safeguarded from evil spirits by the
warning chime that stands at his head. He is suddenly awakened by the ringing of the chimes, and
finds Coreb stealthily approaching to carry him off
to hell. Seeing that the Prologue drew aside the
tiring-house curtains at the beginning to reveal the
recumbent man, it is obvious that the scene must
have been acted on the inner stage, and, if we assume
that Fabel lay with his feet towards the groundlings,
so that he could face the bulk of the audience when
speaking, the chimes must have been placed at the
back of his bed, a position where they could easily
have been rung by a crouching man.

Other bells as well as chimes fell within the
category of stage properties, and among these must
be reckoned the watchman or crier's large handbell,
which, as the frontispiece to Dekker's tract, *The
Belman of London*, reveals, was not only carried but
likewise fastened securely to the waist by a rope.
This bell figures in *The Dutch Courtezan* and in *If It
be not Good, the Divel is in It*, Cockledemoy wielding
it vigorously in the one and Scumbroth in the other.
Much more employed was the table-bell, which
had a considerable variety of uses. We hear it
sounding for breakfast in the second act of *Every
Man in His Humour*, but it must not be taken on that

score as the precursor of the dinner gong. The real
prototype of the dinner gong was the cook's habit of
"knocking to the dresser", to which reference is
made in Suckling's poem, *The Wedding*:

> Just in the nick the cook knock'd thrice,
> And all the waiters in a trice
> Her summons did obey;
> Each serving-man, with dish in hand,
> March'd boldly up, like our train'd band,
> Presented, and away.

"Knocking to the dresser", otherwise, in Cow-
ley's phrase, "The Cook's Drum", was illusively
introduced into several old plays, notably Massinger's
The Unnatural Combat and Fletcher and Shirley's
The Night Walker. Usually the table-bell had other
services. In Brome's *The Covent Garden Weeded*, a
vintner rings it off the stage in the second act to
summon his drawers. Other plays, such as Davenant's *News from Plymouth*, reveal that lawyers were
accustomed to keep a table-bell at their elbow in
their private offices to ring, when necessary, for their
clerks. There was much employment of this acces-
sory in that stirring old Globe play, *The Divil's
Charter*, and the direction for its use in the fourth act,
"he tinketh on a bell", apparently implies that it was
a fixture on a stand, and struck, not rung.

Front-door bells were known in Shakespeare's

time, but by no means commonly provided. It is to
be noted that when one of the permanent doors at
the back of the old platform stage is made to do duty
for the front door of a house, the caller generally
knocks. That the provision of the bell was uncommon is indicated by the story told in the fifth act of
Chapman's *All Fools* of a complaisant husband and
a wanton wife, how the poor man made "a backe-
doore to his house for convenience, gott a bell to his
fore doore, and had an odd fashion in ringing by
which she (his wife) and her maid knew him, and
would stand talking to his next neighbour to prolong
time, that all thinges might be ridde cleanly out-a-
the-way before he came, for the credit of his wife".
As a matter of fact, front-door bells were mostly to
be found in private houses of public resort, namely,
such as were occupied by quacks, astrologers and
prostitutes. In Elizabethan plays they were often to
be heard ringing, but never, I think, seen to be rung.
The instance already cited from *The Golden Age* can
hardly be adjudged an exception.

   To us now this unseen ringing of the door-bell
seems a superfluous bit of realism, but it was an
effective way of heralding a newcomer, seeing that it
permitted of the announcement of a person before
his appearance; added to which it helped to create
atmosphere by localising the action. Take the

situation well on in *Englishmen for my Money*, where
Pisaro is at home on the eve of his daughters' wed-
dings and anxious to keep out intruders. While giving
certain household instructions he is interrupted by
the ringing of the front-door bell, and continues:

> Stay, Frisco, see who rings: look to the door,
> Let none come in, I charge, were he my father:
> I'll keep them whilst I have them: Frisco, who
>   is it?
>
> *Frisco.* She is come in faith.
> *Pisa.* Who is come?
> *Frisco.* Mistress Sushsunce, Mistress Moore's daughter.
> *Pisa.* Mistress Susan, ass? Oh, she must come in.
> *Frisco.* (aside) Hang him, if he keep out a wench.

The supposed Susan, however, is none other than
Walgrave in woman's clothes, and Pisaro, failing to
detect the imposture, the outworks of his citadel are
taken.

Other instances of the same illusion, none perhaps
so effective but all striking faint notes of realism, are
to be found in the opening scene of *The Alchemist*,
the fourth act of *The Bloody Brother*, and in Dekker's
undivided play, *If It be not Good, the Divel is in It*.
That the Elizabethan house-bell was rung by pulling
a rope, much after the manner followed in *The
Golden Age*, is revealed by an episode in the second
act of *Northward Hoe*. Doll, the demirep, on hearing
the welcome sound of the bell, says to her pretended

servants, "Peace, somebody rings! Run, both, whilst he has the rope in's hands; if he be a prize, hale him, if a man-a'war, blow him up, or hang him out at the main-yard's end". And Hans Van Belch, being deemed a prize, is duly captured and brought into harbour.

Undoubtedly, the pleasantest chiming of all in the olden days came from the leashes of tiny globular bells borne by both hobby-horse and man in the often-introduced morris dance. But it had no dramatic significance and could be given none. To acquire that quality, tintinnabulation of the sort had to await the coming of Henry Irving and his memorable presentment of a certain Alsatian innkeeper who was retributively haunted by the jingle of sleigh-bells.

Chapter VIII

THE EVOLUTION OF THE
TRAGIC CARPET

In that deliciously ironical book of etiquette (first published in 1609, but bearing internal evidence of having been written some years earlier), *The Guls Hornbooke*, Dekker has a revealing chapter on "How a Gallant should behave in a Playhouse", which begins with the instruction:

> Whether therefore the gatherers of the publique or private Play-house stand to receive the afternoones rent, let our Gallant (having paid it) presently advance himselfe up to the Throne of the Stage. I meane not the Lords roome (which is now but the Stages suburbs):
> ...But on the very Rushes where the Comedy is to daunce, yea, and under the state of *Cambises* himselfe, must our fethered *Estridge*, like a piece of Ordnance, be planted valiantly (because impudently) beating downe the mewes and hisses of the opposed rascality.

Afterwards, the budding man-about-town is particularly warned that it is not reckoned good form to show any vivid interest in the play. The height of fashion is to pull a wry face and depart disgustedly in the middle:

> No matter whether the Scenes be good or no; the

better they are the worse do you distast them: and, beeing on your feet, sneake not away like a coward, but salute all your gentle acquaintance, that are spread either on the rushes, or on stooles about you, and draw what troope you can from the stage after you.

It is curious that while it has long been a commonplace of stage history that the boards in Shakespeare's day were covered with rushes, no one has troubled to inquire how the custom arose. The regular strewing of rooms in this way in private houses can hardly have afforded an impelling precedent, though it shows that there must have been a ready supply. Nor can it be postulated that the practice arose from considerations of the stage spectator's comfort. The players were better pleased when the gallant paid an extra sixpence for his stool than when he contented himself by lolling on the rushes. Moreover, there is some reason to believe that the practice began long before stage-haunting became a fashionable fad. Primarily, it would appear to have been a necessary precaution. In the days when tragedies and chronicle histories were regular theatrical features, the players had to take many a backfall, and it was essential that their rich and costly dresses should be protected from dust and dirt. There is a hint of this in Nash's *Summer's Last Will and Testament*, which was not an ordinary theatre play and was acted privately by boys in 1592. Summer rebukes the players with:

> You might have written on the margin of your playbook, "Let there be a few rushes in the place where Back Winter shall tumble, for fear of 'wraying his clothes'": or set down "Enter Backwinter with his boy bringing a brush after him, to take off the dust, if need require". But you will ne'er have any wardrobe wit while you live.

Doubtless, the common players had gained wardrobe wit by experience. There are many points on which the stage tells its own story, and the use of rushes is one of them. There is an abundance of evidence, covering a wide period, to show that dramatists always reckoned on their presence as they wrote. What is important to note is that that implies the persistence of the custom in public and private theatres alike, and affords us a corrective to a perplexing simile in *Troilus and Cressida* which seemingly conveys the idea of bare boards:

> And like a strutting player, whose conceit
> Lies in his hamstring, and doth think it rich
> To hear the wooden dialogue and sound
> 'Twixt his stretched footing and the scaffoldage.

As a scaffold was, and is, a temporary platform, it may be that Shakespeare here was thinking of some country stroller strutting on a hastily rigged-up

7-2

stage of boards and barrels. One cannot well apply the description to the London theatres of his time. Does not his own Glendower, when acting as interpreter, say, "She bids you on the wanton rushes lay you down"?[1] In the fourth act of that mysterious end-of-the-century play, *Sir Thomas More*, there is an allusion which certainly implies the presence of rushes on the stage. More has sent ten angels to Witt by a serving man in recompense to the players for their work, and the man has handed over only eight of them. Witt learns of the pilferage, and when Sir Thomas enters, pretends to be looking for something on the floor. More asks him what he is seeking, and Witt slyly replies, "Nay, nothing; your lordship sent eight angills by your man, and I have lost two of them in the rushes".

That the practice was not confined to the public theatres, sundry references in private-theatre plays show. In the opening scene of Middleton and Dekker's *Blurt Master Constable*, as produced at Paul's, we find Fontinel saying after the interrupted dance:

> Lady, bid him whose heart no sorrow feels
> Tickle the rushes with his wanton heels:
> I have too much lead in mine.

So too, in *The Dumb Knight*, a Whitefriars play

[1] *1 Henry VI*, act III, sc. 1, l. 214.

of a slightly later period, Cypres is to be found saying in the opening scene of the fourth act:

> Thou dancest on my heart, lascivious Queene,
> Even as upon these rushes which thou treadest.[1]

It is noteworthy that, although the stage was regularly strewn with rushes, realism sometimes demanded that it should be in part restrewn during the action. It was customary in Elizabeth's reign and after when a distinguished stranger came to a house to lay down fresh rushes in his honour. One finds this practice followed in Chapman's *The Gentleman Usher*, II, I, where Bassiolo gives instructions to the servants as to the proper way to lay down rushes, "in fine smooth threaves"; and again later in Fletcher's *Valentinian*, II, 3, where Phorba says:

> Where is this stranger? Rushes, ladies, rushes!
> Rushes as green as summer for this stranger.

A similar desire for accuracy of detail led to a remarkable innovation at the Globe in 1613, just at the time that historic house was burnt to the ground. Sir Henry Wotton, in a letter written to his nephew giving him particulars of this calamity, reveals that Shakespeare's *Henry VIII* was being acted when it happened. "The King's players", he says, "had a

---

[1] Cf. Field's *Amends for Ladies*, II, 2, "I not esteem him truly as this rush".

new play, called *All is True*, representing some principal pieces of the reign of Henry VIII, which was set forth with many extraordinary circumstances of pomp and majesty, even to the matting of the stage."[1] This innovation was in keeping with the fact that in the great mansions of Jacobean England it was customary to cover the floor of the principal room with Bedfordshire mats made of broad-leaved rushes and coarsely plaited.[2] But, whether or not the burning down of the theatre made the players superstitious about departing from old custom, practically no change in routine took place. The rush-strewn stage remained a characteristic until the downfall of the theatres. In Fletcher's *Rollo, Duke of Normandy*, an early Caroline play, we find the Duke saying early in the second act:

And all my vows my weakness made, like this—
Like this poor heartless rush I rend a-pieces.

In a word, the Elizabethan stage's own testimony about itself is borne out by Flecknoe in his *Short Treatise on the English Stage*, written in 1664:

Now for the difference betwixt our theatres and those of former times, they were but plain and simple, with no other scenes nor decorations of the stage, but only Tapestry, and the Stage strew'd with Rushes (with their habits accordingly).

[1] E. K. Chambers, *The Elizabethan Stage*, II, p. 419.
[2] *Shakespeare's England*, II, pp. 124 and 128.

Relative to this strewing, there remains one other item of evidence which calls for comment in order to preclude any miscomprehension of its import. There has come down to us a somewhat cryptic note of the agreement entered into between the proprietors of Salisbury Court Theatre and its players in September 1639, in which it is indicated that the proprietors had consented to defray half the expense incurred "for rushes, flowers and strowings on the stage".[1] To infer from this that flowers were mingled with the rushes or that some other means were occasionally employed to cover the stage except by rushes would be erroneous. What we have to recall is that, now and again, there was special strewing in the course of the action. Following social custom, flowers were thrown down on the path to be traversed by a returning bridal party. Examples of this are to be found at the opening of two old plays, *The Two Maids of More-clacke* and *The Two Noble Kinsmen*, and in the latter the song "Roses their sharp spines being gone" refers to the strewing.

It is interesting to speculate as to the method pursued at Court performances in pre-Restoration days of covering the bare boards: that is, assuming they were covered—evidence on the point is scanty.

[1] *Shakespeare Society Papers*, IV, p. 99.

Investigation of the matter is in no wise complicated by the fact that Whitehall had no permanent theatre until the meridian of Charles I's reign. We know considerably more about the systems of staging adopted in the Court masques than we do about the systems followed in Court plays, and, although the fundamental principles of the play and the masque were different, it may be that to some slight extent certain conclusions are analogically deducible from masque procedure. The old Revels Accounts reveal that it was customary to cover the dancing place in front of the stage and the scaffolds for spectators with green cloth, and, although nothing is said directly about the stage, it may be inferred that it was covered in the same way. Of the expense thus incurred, at a time when money had many times its present purchasing power, we have a record in a payment for two performances in the Christmas of 1613–14:

To Richard Ansell Matteyer to his Ma[ty] upon Warrant dated 22 June 1614 for his paines and chardges in nayling downe the greene clothe in the Banquetting House at severall times for the Maske performed before his Ma[ty] at Christmas last past...vii li. ix s. iiij d.[1]

In following up this clue, I met with some

[1] Peter Cunningham, *Revels Accounts* (1842), p. xliv. Cf. Reyher, *Les Masques Anglais*, p. 358 note 5.

interesting but not wholly satisfying results. There is proof that the Court stage in the final years of Queen Elizabeth had some sort of covering, but there is no precise indication of its nature. It is well recognised by scholars that the sole text we have of Dekker's *Old Fortunatus*—the quarto of 1600—is the special Court version of the play as given at Whitehall on December 27, 1599. The play is undivided, but in act I, sc. 3, according to the modern division, there is an elaborate description of the masque of Vice, Fortune and Virtue. Two trees are brought on, the tree of Virtue and the tree of Vice. Fortune says:

> You ministers of Virtue, Vice and Fortune,
> Tear off this upper garment of the earth,
> And in her naked bosom stick those trees.

Then comes the direction, "Whilst the Priest sings, the rest set the trees in the earth". Firmly planted, the trees remained on the stage until the end of the play. Early in the fourth act, Andelocia, at Agripyne's urging, climbs the tree of Vice to gather apples. It is difficult to get away from the impression that Fortune's command, "Tear off this upper garment of the earth", implies the removal of some sort of covering. Green cloth would have been appropriate, but, if it were used, it must have been laid down in strips.

In a former study of *The Tempest*, I advanced some reasons for believing that the incidental masque as we now have it was not originally in the play but was specially written for the Court performance of 1613, given in celebration of the betrothal of the Lady Elizabeth and the Prince Palatine.[1] Consideration of my present subject has since revealed to me some evidence which apparently supports that contention. Iris, in the masque, when summoning Ceres, says Juno bids her:

> Here, on this grass-plot, in this very place,
> To come and sport.

Ceres, on appearing, asks:

> ...why hath thy queen
> Summon'd me hither, to this short-grass'd green?

And, later on, Iris, in calling up the naiades, commands them to:

> Leave your crisp channels, and on this green land,
> Answer your summons.

Why all this iteration about the colour of the locality, and especially the reference to "this short-grass'd green"? Does it not appear that the writer of the masque, whether Shakespeare or another (a moot point), had a green stage cloth in his mind's eye when composing it?

[1] See "The masque in *The Tempest*" in *The Fortnightly Review* for June 1920.

Whatever may have been the earlier practice, there are certainly good grounds for believing that in Caroline days at least the Court stage was regularly covered with green cloth. Otherwise, we should hardly find the same course pursued at Court from the earliest days of the Restoration, in fact, from November 1660.[1] There, indeed, the practice held good until the end of the century. On this score the Lord Chamberlain's books are remarkably revealing. We learn of the purchase from time to time of "green baize lined with canvas, to cover the stage", and once of many yards of "grasse green Manchester baize" (an item which recalls the phrasing in *The Tempest*). So far from being permanently nailed down, the covering was readily removable, an arrangement which prevented rapid deterioration. In 1667, the Court upholsterer sent in a bill "for making a false Cover for the stage, to fasten with iron buttons".

Precedent for the Restoration Court stage might be readily and reasonably surmised, but precedent for the academic stage of the period, where the same custom obtained, cannot well be suggested. For the performance of *Nola* at Trinity College, Cambridge, in 1668, "sixteen yards of green bays" were

[1] Eleanore Boswell, *The Restoration Court Stage*, p. 300, appendix E, "Green baize for the stage".

purchased "to cover ye stage".[1] But the truth is that all stages alike at this period, whether public or private, had exactly the same covering. So far, however, as the ordinary Restoration theatres are concerned, this fact now remains to be established. Clun, the popular Drury Lane actor, was murdered by highway robbers while returning from the country on the night of August 2, 1664. Shortly afterwards an elegiac broadside was issued presenting the following quaint entreaty:

Mourn, Royal Stage, your Poets' pens implore,
To cease to write, since Clun can be no more;
Turn all your Sceans to black, and let them be
The Emblemes of our cares: Clun's Tragedy;
Go hide your Tapestry, and Clothes of Green,
Act now on black, Clun will no more be seen.[2]

The testimony of strangers within the gate enables us to substantiate what is here merely implied. Samuel de Sorbières, writing in 1664 of his recent English experiences, says:

Le Théâtre est fort beau, couvert d'un Tapis verd, et en scène y est toute libre, avec beaucoup de changemens, et des perspectives.[3]

[1] Malone Society Collections, II, pt. 2, p. 178.
[2] G. Thorn-Drury, A Little Ark of Seventeenth Century Verse, p. 30.
[3] Relation d'un voyage en Angleterre, Paris, 1664. I regret to say that this passage was formerly misinterpreted in my The Elizabethan Playhouse and Other Studies, First Series, pp. 188-9.

By "en scène y est toute libre" he means not encumbered with spectators, as in Paris. So, too, M. de Monconys, in describing a visit paid to the Theatre Royal, Bridges Street, otherwise Drury Lane, on May 22, 1663, writes:

L'après-dinée nous fusmes chez le Milord de S. Alban, et de là à la Comédie dans la loge du Roy. Le Théâtre est le plus propre et le plus beau que j'aye jamais veu, tout tapissé par le bas de bayette verte; aussi bien que toutes les loges qui en sont tapissés avec des bandes de cuir doré.[1]

Since the Restoration playhouses might almost be described as Court appanages, so largely did they depend upon old Rowley and his courtiers for support, it would appear that in establishing the principle of the green cloth they were influenced by Court practice. My idea is that the convention held good for a score of years only, and was finally discarded owing to the increasing demands of spectacle. Profuse trapwork, the ascent of elaborate set pieces from the cellar (such as the Cave of Proteus in *Albion and Albanius* in 1685), was incompatible with a permanent covering. At an earlier period, the stage had no more than two small traps for apparitions, and both were situated on the apron, otherwise the part of the stage in front of the curtain.

[1] *Journal des Voyages de Monsieur de Monconys*, Lyon, 1666, pt. II, p. 25.

But this was not the end of the story. So far from wholly disappearing, the green cloth merely shrunk in its dimensions and, being given a particular use, had at last a particular significance. Its preservation was due to the necessity which had first brought the stage rushes into use, the need to protect the players' costumes from dust and dirt, an office which confined its services to tragedy. From a period early in the eighteenth century, the practice was, immediately before the death of one of the characters, for two men to come openly on the stage carrying the cloth which it was their business to spread out. When this began can only be approximated, but there is a record of "The Stage cloth" in an inventory of the scenery, properties and other articles stored in the Theatre Royal, Covent Garden, early in 1744, now preserved in the British Museum.[1]

This obtrusive spreading of the tragic carpet, as it came to be called, had its disadvantages. As Goldsmith pointed out in the first number of *The Bee* in 1759, and iterated in *The Citizen of the World* (Letter XXI), climax was often forestalled by the coming on of the two scenemen with their burden. Moreover, the carpet lent itself to ludicrous happenings. John O'Keeffe, in his *Recollections*, tells a

---

[1] Add. MS. 12,201, reproduced in part in Henry Saxe Wyndham's *Annals of Covent Garden Theatre*, II, p. 309.

humorous story relative to the miscasting in a tragic rôle at the Crow Street Theatre, Dublin, in 1773, of Robert Mahon, a vocal comedian:

The first night that Murphy's *Grecian Daughter* was performed in Dublin, Mahon played Dionysius, the tyrant. It was the ridiculous custom at that time, when the principal character was to die, for two men to walk on with a carpet and spread it on the stage for the hero to fall on and die in comfort. Dionysius was stabbed and had to expire. Mahon fell upon the carpet and began his dying speech. Possessed with full inspiration from the Tragic Muse, he grinned and frothed, and threw his eyes around and about, and grasped the carpet with both hands, and writhed and twisted, speaking all the time, by which means, before his speech was half finished, he had wrapped himself so tightly up in this tragic table-cloth of Melpomene, that nothing could be seen of him but the tip of his nose, red with fury.

Evidently this was not the first time something of the sort had occurred. There is an episode in the Spouting Club scene in the second act of *The Apprentice*, a popular Drury Lane farce dating from 1755, which reads like a burlesque of Mahon's antics. Despite the manifold absurdities of the convention, mere theatrical utility kept it long in vogue, even after the stage itself had come to make open mock at it. Here is what Garrick put into Mrs Barry's mouth,

when she came in 1778 to deliver his epilogue to
Home's tragedy of *Alfred*:

> If this green cloth could speak, would it not tell,
> Upon its well-worn nap, how oft I fell?
> To death in various forms delivered up:
> Steel kills me one night, and the next the cup.

There came a time, however, about the end of the
century when the illusion-marring and anticipative
attributes of the convention could be no longer
tolerated, but even then the players could not bring
themselves wholly to abandon the green cloth.
Without knowing it, they reverted to Restoration
principles. The cloth resumed its pristine dimensions
and covered the boards from first to last when
tragedy was in the bill. Hazlitt, in reviewing a
performance of *The Revenge* given at Drury Lane in
October 1817, complained that Rae, the Alonzo,
stamped about so hard that he raised "not only a
shout in the upper gallery, but a cloud of dust from
the green baize on the stage floor". So far was the
old green cloth looked upon as an essential con-
comitant of tragedy that when necessity demanded
or accident occasioned its absence, critics deplored
the defection; and, by a parity of reasoning, they
resented its use otherwise than in tragedy. In its
issue of March 2, 1821, the trenchant little *Dublin
Theatrical Observer* has a notice of the performance of

Romeo and Juliet at the new Theatre Royal on the night previous, in which it was remarked that:

There was no green cloth spread upon the stage— perhaps this was lest it should interfere with the movements of the dancers in the Masquerade scene. We, however, should like to know what colourable pretext the Manager has for withholding this and the *Green Curtain*, unless it be to shew an utter contempt for public opinion.

The same journal, in criticising the performance of *Love in a Village* four days later, says:

Upon our entering the Theatre, we were somewhat surprised at seeing the Stage covered with a green cloth, and naturally imagined that the performance had from some unforeseen cause been changed to a tragedy, and it was not until the Duet commenced between Rosetta and Lucinda that we were convinced that the piece was to be, as advertised; however, at the close of the act, when the Statute Fair commenced, we saw at once that the Manager was anxious to make the scene appear as natural as possible by supplying the imitation of a green sward for the dancers; this is novel, and it only wanted a pair of stocks upon the Green to look *vastly rural.*

These extracts show it was seldom safe in the old days to flout the conventions. The green baize was now a well recognised tragic symbol, and so long remained. In his memorable essay on the death of Elliston, written in 1831, Charles Lamb said:

AN   8

He carried about with him his pit, boxes and galleries, and set up his portable playhouse at the corners of streets and in the market places. Upon flintiest pavements he trod the boards still; and if his theme chanced to be passionate, the green baize carpet of tragedy spontaneously rose beneath his feet.

Once more, however, the old green cloth shrivelled up. By 1856, it had come to occupy a space where it could not interfere with the scene-shifting, that is to say, between the footlights and the first entrance. In February of that year, the editor of *The Theatrical Journal*, in reply to a correspondent, wrote, "we do not object in the least to the green baize, for it has become such a matter of use with us, that if it were dispensed with, we should scarcely believe that a tragedy was about to be represented". But the convention was moribund and the taste for tragedy itself declining. Like most old customs, it was to make its last stand in the country, but within three years it had ceased to be observed on the London stage.

Chapter IX

BYGONE STAGE FURNITURE AND ITS REMOVERS

Plain facts are not always easy to realise. It is difficult for the playgoer of to-day to imagine that there was a time in the history of the secular drama when the property-man was non-existent, and when there were neither stage hands nor stage accessories. Yet there was a stretch of fifty years beginning in the last decade of the fifteenth century when this was the case. Written for no more than three or four players, the primitive interlude was a trifling piece designed to be given (as its name originally betokened) on the floor of a banqueting hall in the midst of a feast. It was quintessential drama, for in the conditions no accessories could be utilised. Even when the interlude developed into the morality and lost its association with eating and drinking, its spartan simplicity of presentation still obtained. There have come down to us at least thirteen pieces of the morality type, such as *Lusty Juventus*, *Wit and Science* and *The Interlude of Youth*, concerning which it may be

8-2

confidently affirmed that no properties were called for in their representation. It was not until tragedy and comedy timidly emerged that any necessity arose for the provision of properties generally and furniture in particular, and the sudden need, at a time when stage hands were undreamed-of luxuries, caused these accessories to be placed in position in a very naïve way. So far from being put on the stage at the beginning of a scene, they were brought in just at the moment when they were required; and it was the business of the playwright (if he could) to rationalise their introduction. Thus, in the third scene of *Calisto and Meliboea*, a rude comedy of the period of 1530, Calisto says to Sempronio, "Go fet me my lute, and bring some chair or stool with thee, the argument of love I may dispute", and Sempronio forthwith obeys. But when the properties were otherwise than furniture, their bringing in could seldom be neatly effected. In that primitive tragedy, *Apius and Virginia*, written about 1560, one finds towards the close an exceedingly quaint direction. It reads, "Doctrina and Memorie and Virginius bring in a tomb".

It is a remarkable fact that this calling for chairs and what not, and their bringing in by characters in the play established itself firmly as a convention, and was persistently followed in the Elizabethan theatres, though not wholly to the exclusion of other methods. Albeit that progress has been well defined as continuity in the midst of change, this carrying over of a primitive principle into a period of stabilisation is certainly curious, seeing that, once the drama had been given permanent housing, there was a betterment of conditions which made for elaboration of detail.

What we have primarily to bear in mind is that, in Shakespeare's day, lack of painted scenery was largely compensated for by the use of furniture. Apart from its aid to the illusion of the moment (and realism was then sedulously sought after where it could be readily obtained), furniture, in the absence of programmes, served a more or less necessary localising purpose. Unhampered by any questions of scene-shifting, the Elizabethan dramatist wrote his play in many scenes; and, with interiors and exteriors often rapidly alternating, dire confusion would have resulted had not some distinction been made between the two. That distinction furniture afforded. But none of it was purely ornamental: nothing was used except what was brought into service during the action. There were two methods of placing it in position, according to the exigencies. Behind the open projecting platform was a small inner stage hidden by a double curtain; and the

furniture of a room could be set on this before the
curtain was drawn. Such a position, however, was
none too good for sight or hearing, and, what was
worse, the chairs and tables seriously restricted the
action. Whence it came that scaffolds for execution
and beds were often thrust out on to the open platform. Apart from occasional use of the inner stage,
furniture was placed in position only a few moments
before it was wanted, and, once it had served its
purpose, it was cleared away. There was good reason
for this. Space for the (often vigorous) action was
limited by the presence of rows of stool-occupying
gallants on either side of the stage.

It has been stated that the illusion of the scene was
never marred in Elizabethan days by this bringing
on and carrying off of furniture, because the hands
employed were always characters in the play,
generally servants with a line or two to speak. This
is no more than a half-truth, and half-truths are
invariably misleading. The carriers were not always
characters in the play. When furniture was wanted
on the open stage at the beginning of a scene or even
later, and the dramatist had omitted to make anyone
call for it, it was brought in and carried out by
regular stage hands commonly known as stage-
keepers or tiremen. But as these men invariably
wore blue coats, the recognised livery of a servant,

their comings and goings rarely proved a disturbing factor.

The advantage in calling for furniture was that the call served as a cue, and ensured that the chairs and tables and what not would be in place exactly when they were required. Examples showing the persistence of this primitive method abound. Thus, in the play-scene in the fourth act of *The Spanish Tragedy*, Hieronimo orders a chair and cushion to be brought in for the King, and Balthazar obeys the command. So too, in *The Miseries of Inforst Marriage*, near the close, when the butler announces Dr Baxter, Scarborow bids him bring in "a table, candles, stools, and all things fit". (For us now to see an Elizabethan play acted wholly in the Elizabethan manner would convey the impression that our forebears lived in unfurnished apartments.) It is to be noted that in the puppet-show scene in the last act of Jonson's *The Tale of a Tub*, no order is given to anybody, but two grooms busy themselves placing ten chairs in position for the coming audience, and gossip as they work.[1]

Often as we find orders being given for the bringing in of furniture, it is much less often that we

[1] For other examples of calling for furniture, see *The Phoenix*, III, I, *The City Madam*, I, 3, and V, 3, and *The Royal King and Loyal Subject*, III, 4.

come across orders for its removal. Nor can these always be taken literally. When old Capulet cries:

> More light, you knaves; and turn the tables up,
> And quench the fire, the room is grown too hot,

he (or rather Shakespeare) is indulging in a bit of verbal scene-painting, for neither tables nor fire are in sight. Usually, however, the stage hands were left to remove the furniture once it had served its purpose, without receiving any open instructions, but there were cases where they could not fittingly act. Not only probability but the proprieties had to be considered. When a lady was shown in a pushed-in bed, and more especially when the lady was leading a cloistered life, as in the instance which follows, it would have been unseemly for men to have done the pushing. In the fourth act of Heywood's *The Golden Age*, the reclining Danae is drawn in and drawn out again by four beldams, her sole attendants in the impregnable tower. Now and again, it is to be remarked, something was neatly said by way of explaining the removal of a thrust-out bed. At the close of the bedroom scene in the last act of *Monsieur Thomas*, the order comes, "Draw in the bed, maids, and see it made again".

Progression in the Elizabethan theatre was expeditious, and the stage hands had to do their work with celerity. No matter how many articles of furniture were brought on at a time, to hold up the traffic of the scene would have been an unpardonable offence. A direction in the fifth act of Heywood's *The Iron Age* shows how swiftness in these matters was attained. It reads: "Enter Thersites with Souldiers, bringing in a table, with chayres and stooles plac'd above it".

There were many occasions, generally at the openings of median scenes, when no order could be fittingly given for the placing in position of needed furniture, and, in such cases, the ordinary stage hands officiated. Shakespeare affords us an example. In *Henry VIII*, at the beginning of the fourth scene in the first act, two tables and a number of stools were brought in openly on the outer stage for only a comparatively brief period. With the announcement of the King's imminence comes the direction, "All rise and tables remov'd".

Revolutionary in a way as the introduction of scenery proved at the Restoration, it did not wholly prevent the continuance of old conventions. For a time, indeed, even the calling for furniture persisted, but only for a time. In the second act of Tuke's *The Adventures of Five Hours*, as produced at the Duke's Theatre in Lincoln's Inn Fields in 1663, there is a scene where Porcia summons an attendant, and says to him,

> Page, bid Mirabel come in and Floridor
> With his lute, and send in some body with chairs.

The ensuing direction conveys that "They bring in chairs", meaning, doubtless, that the ordinary stage hands did the work. Curiously enough, while the time-honoured practice of calling for furniture soon ceased, the office of open furniture-remover remained for close on another two centuries. Theatrically speaking, with all the choppings and changings, there was only one hand-clasp between Shakespeare and Edmund Kean. It needs to recall that in Restoration days the Elizabethan stock of plays still continued to be drawn upon, and new plays, so far from being fashioned to cause as little scene-shifting as possible, were still written in acts of many (sometimes half a dozen) scenes. Much might have been done to minimise the necessity of bringing on and bearing off furniture had a sensible use been made of the newly introduced front curtain; but the full helpfulness of that auxiliary was long in dawning upon the players, as evidenced by the fact that it did not begin to drop regularly between the acts until the middle of the eighteenth century.

In the circumstances, it is not at all surprising that

in Restoration days not even what was presented as the most luxurious of salons was ever more than meagrely furnished. Rarely was the provision more than a table and a couple or so of chairs. When anything more elaborate was required to give the necessary local colour, it was painted on the scene. Suggestion, rather than realism, being the aim, illusion was not marred by this quaint expedient. An example comes to hand in the second act of Orrery's *The Black Prince*, as acted at the Theatre Royal in 1667, wherein one of the directions reads: "The scene opens and Francisco appears in a magical habit (with his closet painted about him with mathematical instruments and grotesque figures)".

Though Otway, Congreve and Cibber had been so far influenced by French observance of the unities as to write some of their plays wholly or partly in single-scene acts, few later authors fell in line. With us, the old Elizabethan go-as-you-please method of construction held good in very considerable measure until the mid-Victorian period. That was why the venerable but wholly unvenerated furniture-remover remained for so long a necessary evil. Most playgoers agreed with Mr Puff in *The Critic* when he said to the scene-men: "It is always awkward, in a tragedy, to have you fellows coming on in your playhouse liveries to remove things. I wish it could be managed better". About the only change that had been made in the practice since Shakespeare's day was in these playhouse liveries, which, from being blue, were now green.

Once upon a time a stage furniture-remover was actually honoured with a round or two of applause, but the circumstances were exceptional. When, by way of giving a fillip to the attractions of *The Beggar's Opera*, Gay's old piece was given at Covent Garden in October 1781 with an entire female cast, including Nan Catley as Captain Macheath and Mrs Webb as Lockit, consistency was maintained by having a furniture-remover of the same sex. A contemporary journal, after dealing with the acting of the principals, ended by saying:

> The rest of the characters, allowing for the change of sexes, were as well as could be expected, not forgetting the female stage attendant, who, from the novelty of bringing on and off chairs, tables, etc., produced almost each time an involuntary burst of applause.

Yet, with this persistence of the old stage hand, the mounting of plays was steadily suffering a sea-change. Already the growing demands for realism necessitated some kinds of apartments being much better furnished than they had been in post-Restoration days. Now and again my lady's chamber was actually provided with a toilette table and a spinet.

The monotony of the regulation two chairs and a table in library scenes was occasionally relieved—as in Reynolds's comedy of *The Dramatist*—by the addition of a sofa. By the end of the century furniture had actually come to form part of the play. In 1797, a correspondent of *The Monthly Mirror*, signing himself "Honestus", wrote complaining that the playwrights of the day were compelled by the prevailing craze to cudgel their brains in devising pantomime tricks rather than on concentrating on plot and characterisation. "Chairs", he moans, "must be broken, tables overturned, candlesticks tossed in the air, screens thrown down."

Since a couple of stage hands were utterly incapable of clearing away the contents of an elaborately furnished room with the necessary dispatch, the question might well be asked, how came it that the old furniture-remover still continued to hold office? The answer is that many interiors were still sparsely furnished, since it was only at certain junctures that elaborate mounting could be indulged in. A realistic scene of this order had to be staged either at the end of an act when the curtain could be dropped upon it, or, if it came intermediately, acted well at the back, so that it could be finally shut off from view by running on a pair of flats in front of it.

Thus it was that the old furniture-remover not

only lived long but travelled far. Jonathan Oldstyle (otherwise Washington Irving), in discussing the characteristics of the New York audience of 1803, says of the "gods" that, amongst other things, "They also have the privilege of demanding a bow from John, (by which name they designate every servant at the theatre who enters to move a table or snuff a candle)". In the English and Irish country theatres of the period worthies of this order seldom were neatly dressed or did their work efficiently. On this score one finds an interesting statement in *The Belfast Newsletter* of December 24, 1813:

We cannot forbear noticing and commending an improvement in one important particular hitherto unknown in the Belfast Theatre. Two boys in livery are in constant attendance to bring in and remove chairs, tables and other articles necessary in a change of scene. They are a genteel appendage seen in the London and Dublin theatres, and since there must be persons to execute the office (for we know of no other means than the hands of servants) it is pleasing to see these well-dressed boys, in lieu of, perhaps, a ragged little being without shoes or stockings, whom we formerly have seen obtrude himself for the purpose.

"Obtrude" is the word, though in using it the scribe wrote better than he knew. Even in the country theatres the claims of realism were growing imperious and soon evoked protests against the

PLATE III

THE
HONORABLE
HISTORIE OF
FRIER *BACON*, AND
FRIER *BONGAY*.

As it was lately plaid by the Prince *Palatine* his Seruants.

Made by *Robert Greene*, Maſter of Arts.

LONDON,
Printed by ELIZABETH ALLDE dwelling
neere Chriſt-Church. 1630.

Title-page of Greene's *Friar Bacon and Friar Bungay*, 1630

constant breaking of the illusion. In an early issue of a little Birmingham sheet called *The Theatrical Looker-On*, published in 1822, Butler, the local stage manager, is asked:

Will you, therefore, inform us why the Scenery continues to be worked so disgracefully; why "he of the crimson breeches" always exhibits his person without his coat; why the "Knight of the paper-cap" always comes on *before* the scene instead of *behind* it; why he who *clears* the stage always contrives to leave himself *on* it; and why all these worthies are heard louder than the actors?

Nor was it in the country alone that audience and players alike were distracted and annoyed by the vagaries of these gentry, especially the green coats, as the furniture-removers still continued to be called. One notes that *The Morning Chronicle*, in its account of the production of Dimond's *The Nymph of the Grotto* at Covent Garden in January 1829, recorded:

Madame Vestris seemed to like her part and was in good humour, excepting when (as deputy stage manager, we conclude) she audibly abused the stage-keepers for removing two chairs that ought to have remained.

As manageress and producer, Madame Vestris was noted for the luxury (perhaps over-elaboration would be the better term) of her interiors; and it is not surprising, viewing the above extract, that she should have striven to get rid of the stage's old-man-of-the-sea. In 1831, at the close of her first managerial season at the Olympic, the whole stage was re-modelled. At intervals of four feet backwards from the footlights the boards were fitted with six traps, all available for every piece played, and up which were sent the properties for each scene, thus avoiding changes in sight of the audience. But it was not until thirty years later, when, thanks to Fechter's mani-fold innovations at the Lyceum, dramatists became impressed with the utility of writing plays wholly in single-scene acts, that any general movement set in in favour of abolishing the time-honoured furniture-remover. Dealing in the issue of *All The Year Round* for October 31, 1863, with Fechter's abortive introduction of the French scenic system, under the optimistic heading of "A New Stage Stride", an anonymous writer said:

The banishing from the boards of that abnormal personage, the stage-footman, with his red breeches and white stockings, is an improvement on which we cannot but congratulate the manager of the Lyceum Theatre. It was not pleasant to sit and watch the proceedings of these gentry during a pause in the drama, though it must be owned that they appeared to know their business better than the footmen of ordinary life. With what precision they used to place the table on which the deed was to be signed, in its exact place; the sofa, again, never had to be removed an inch after it was once put down; the very footstools seemed to be attracted to their right places as if by magnetic force. Still, those footmen used to give one a shock, and bring one's imagination down to the realities of life whenever they appeared, and it is agreeable to think that in future their work will be accomplished by means of trap-doors and other simple contrivances.

But it was idle to write as if this were the end. The swallow had heralded the summer, not brought it. Obsolescent the old furniture-remover undoubtedly was, but country air prolonged his life for a considerable number of years.

Chapter X

BACON ON MASQUES AND TRIUMPHS

Nothing that Bacon ever wrote is better known than his essay "On Masques and Triumphs", and nothing of his has been so ill-comprehended. On this score, scholarship has the right to sit in sackcloth and ashes. Appositely enough, there comes to mind a curiously prophetic passage in *The Advancement of Learning*:

> Let us consider the false appearances that are imposed on us by words, which are framed and applied according to the conceit and capacities of the vulgar sort; and although we think we govern our words, and prescribe it well *loquendum ut vulgus sentiendum ut sapientis*; yet certain it is that words, as a Tartar's bow, do shoot back upon the understanding of the wisest.

Strange, is it not, that, although Bacon himself sedulously governed his words, Aldis Wright would have us believe that he began his essay infelicitously by giving it a pleonastic title. Basing on an ill-considered premiss, he maintains in a note on *A Midsummer Night's Dream*, I, I, 19, that the essay treats of masques alone, and that, consequently, "masques" and "triumphs" are synonymous terms. This is absurd. Bacon deals specifically with Triumphs in his final paragraph:

> For justs, and tourneys and barriers, the glories of them are chiefly in the chariots, wherein the challengers make their entry; especially if they be drawn with strange beasts; as lions, bears, camels and the like; or in the devices of their entrance, or in bravery of their liveries, or in the goodly furniture of their horses and armour. But enough of these toys.

There are occasions when the best sort of gloss is a pictorial gloss: it conveys in a glance what a long description may fail to make clear. Yet how seldom is anything of the sort employed. Seeing how plainly it reveals that barriers were indoor tilting, the most informing commentary on this passage would be a reproduction of Jacques Callot's series of plates entitled "Combat à la Barrière faict en cour de Lorraine le 14 Fébvrier en l'année présente, 1627".

No one of his day could speak more authoritatively on masques than Bacon. He himself had written one as early as 1595, and he had been concerned with their production at Gray's Inn and at Whitehall, on and off, for a score of years. But, since the early seventeenth-century masque was rapid in its develop-

ment and underwent many changes, it is essential
to bear in mind the precise period when his essay
was published. Otherwise, it is impossible to
determine how much he knew about masque
production when he wrote, or to trace with any
accuracy the particular performances which he
praised or dispraised. Though in all likelihood
drafted at a somewhat earlier period, the essay was
first given to the world in 1625, when it formed
No. xxxvii of the considerably augmented third
edition of the *Essays*. By that time Bacon had
witnessed most of the developments the masque
was fated to undergo. Hardly anything of any
particular newness was to follow except a marked
approximation in arrangement to the French Court
ballet, a change which took place in late Caroline
days and was due to the predilections of Henrietta
Maria and her train. In Bacon's boyhood, the typical
Court masque was no more than a series of dances
preluded by a monologue of merely personal significance. He had watched that monologue develop until
it had become, under the guiding genius of Ben
Jonson and Inigo Jones, a delightful lyric fantasy
with quasi-dramatic qualities, relieved by comic
episode, and enriched by scenic ornament. Already
it had heralded the public coming of the modern
picture stage.

One reason why we require to bear in mind the date of the essay's publication is that it enables us to determine how much truth there is in the charge that in it Bacon evinces a narrow partiality. Some years ago that charge was made and re-made by one of the most distinguished of Shakespearian scholars, Edward Dowden, who betrayed thereby an astonishing ignorance of the history and fundamental characteristics of the masque.[1] Taking his cue from Spedding, Dowden maintained that the essay "consists of little else than indirect commendation" of Beaumont's *Masque of the Inner Temple and Gray's Inn* (which formed one of the features of the royal wedding celebrations at Whitehall in February 1613, and in whose production Bacon had interested himself), "and censure of the rival masque of the *Middle Temple and Lincoln's Inn*". Admitted that some of the points in the essay apply to these two masques, though rarely to one or other alone, the charge is ill-grounded; once the evidence on which Dowden bases is scrutinised it proves illusive. Remarkably enough, he made no examination of the third masque given at this juncture—Campion's *The Lords' Masque*—though it was the first in order

[1] Article on "The English masque" in *The Nineteenth Century* for July 1899; reprinted in the author's *Essays Modern and Elizabethan*, 1910.

and presented on the Princess Elizabeth's wedding
night. Yet, as I shall have occasion to show, one of
the features he finds praised in Beaumont's masque
figured more prominently in its predecessor. Even
if we assume that petty jealousies arose in 1613
between the temporarily allied Inns of Court, these
would surely have disappeared long before 1625. A
comprehensive essay on masques published in that
year could hardly have been confined to old and
fleeting issues. With Inigo Jones's dominance and
his steady advance towards an ever-receding goal,
progress had been unceasing; and Bacon's wise saws
would have had little cogency had they not been
based on modern instances.

To mention without comment certain masque
features which happen to be features of a masque
with which one was personally connected is not to
indulge in oblique commendation of that masque.
It is true that Bacon maintains that the colours of
costumes which show best by candlelight are white,
carnation and a kind of sea-water green, and that
these colours were seen (though not all in combination) in Beaumont's masque. But it is surely not
pretended that all or any of them were then first
used in masque-costuming. Note that in Jonson's
Masque of Beauty in 1608, "the colours of the masquers were varied; the one half in orange-tawny and

silver; *the other in sea-green and silver"*. Dowden is apparently on safer ground when he sees in the following passage a stricture on Chapman's *Masque of the Middle Temple and Lincoln's Inn*:

> It is true, the alteration of scenes, so it be quietly and without noise, are things of great beauty and pleasure; for they feed and relieve the eye before it be full of the same object.

Unless we can conceive that Bacon was recalling a certain episode in Chapman's masque, it is difficult to see why he indulged in so ugly a phrase as "quietly and without noise". There were two kinds of noises heard in association with the shifting of scenery in the Stuart masques, the fortuitous and the intentional, the former usual, the latter not; and Bacon's meaning might be clearer if we read "without deliberate noise". Ordinarily there was apt to be so much creaking of the rude machinery in bringing about these visual transformations that it was customary to drown the disagreeable sounds in a flood of music. Chapman, on the other hand, deliberately resorted to noise in his masque to obtain a *coup de théâtre*: one of the reasons why, in all probability, it was considered as more of the nature of a play than a masque. A mountain scene, after being first revealed, moved slightly forward and opened without a loud crack. Assuming that

Bacon censured this cheap effect, it cannot be taken otherwise than honest criticism. He was careful to see that as little noise as possible was made in the masques with which he was directly associated. In *The Masque of Flowers*, a Gray's Inn Court entertainment of Christmas, 1613, which was got up under his superintendence and at his expense, we read of certain set-pieces representing banks of flowers "softly descending and vanishing".

A sentence or two earlier there is censure of wider application and much greater severity. "Turning dances into figure", says Bacon, "is a childish curiosity." Judging by its persistence, it was a curiosity not easily sated. So far back as 1606 there had been seen in Jonson's *Masque of Hymen* a dance in which the masquers occasionally grouped themselves into letters "very signifying to the name of the bridegroom", and ended by forming a symbolical chain subsequently expounded by Reason. Other devices of the sort formed features of *The Masque of Queens* (1609) and *Cupid's Banishment* (1617). The truth is that Bacon's strictures, so far from betraying petty bias, are wholly dispassionate. The lash sometimes falls on himself. Rich embroidery he condemns as useless extravagance, though he cannot have forgotten that the masquers in *The Masque of Flowers* had doublets "richly embroidered

PLATE IV

Callot's etching of a scene in the *Liberatione di Tirreno*, as performed in the Ducal Palace at Florence in 1616.

(Showing the method of masque performance pursued at the Jacobean and Caroline Courts.)

in curious panes with embossed flowers of silver, the panes bordered with embroidery of carnations, silk and silver". Moreover, one can as readily find indirect censure as indirect commendation of Beaumont's masque. It would lie in the following reflection:

Some sweet odours suddenly coming forth, *without any drops falling*, are, in such a company as there is steam and heat, things of great pleasure and refreshment.

In other words, Bacon preferred "the mist made of delicate perfumes" out of which Truth and Opinion emerged when *The Barriers* of rare old Ben was given at Whitehall on Twelfth Night, 1606, to the shower of perfumed rain[1] which fell in Beaumont's masque when Iris besought the aid of Flora in return for favours given. There is no partiality here.

In writing of anti-masques, Bacon says, "But chiefly, let the music of them be recreative, and with some strange changes". Dowden sees in this oblique commendation of Beaumont's first anti-masque, overlooking the fact that it applies more closely to the anti-masque of lunatics in Campion's preceding

[1] For which see the *Calendar of State Papers, Venetian*, 1610–13, pp. 532–3, Foscarini's letter of May 10, 1613, to the Doge of Venice. No mention of this shower occurs in the printed masque.

masque. After Orpheus in this bids music "put on Protean changes", the official description of the ensuing action reads:

> At the sound of a strange music twelve Frantics enter, six men and six women, all presented in sundry habits and humours. There was the lover, the self-lover, the melancholic-man full of fear...with others that made an absolute medley of madness; in the midst of whom Entheus (or Poetic Fury) was hurried forth, and tost up and down, till by virtue of a new change in the music, the lunatics fell into a mad measure, fitted to a loud fantastic tune; but in the end thereof the music changed into a very solemn air, which they softly played, while Orpheus spake.

Reminiscences of Beaumont's masque in Bacon's essay there undoubtedly are—the reference to "statuas moving" is unmistakable—but Dowden, in pursuit of his chimera, finds them where they are not. Contrary to his opinion, there is no dancing to song with or without apposite ditty in the Inner Temple and Gray's Inn masque, nothing to which allusion could have been made in the passage:

> Dancing to song is a thing of great state and pleasure. I understand it that the song be in quire, placed aloft, and accompanied with some broken music; and the ditty fitted to the device.

Here Dowden has misinterpreted Beaumont's somewhat ambiguous final direction:

The Knights dance their parting measure, and ascend, put on their swords and belts; during which time the Priests sing the fifth and last song.

This last song, sung in quire but certainly not "aloft", consists of a single eight-line stanza, of a surety insufficient to answer for the masquers' parting measure and their ascent from the dancing place to the stage. Careful study of what precedes reveals that "during which time" means while the Knights return to the stage and resume their discarded trappings. First, the priests descend and sing a brief song while the Knights come down to the floor of the Banqueting House. A second equally brief song follows the Knights' dancing of their first measure, and songs are given after the three ensuing dances. There is no vocal accompaniment to the dancing: the singing is merely for breathing space and to lend dignity and impressiveness to the coming and going of the Knights.

Even supposing that Dowden is right and I am wrong, Bacon cannot be taken here as singling out Beaumont's masque for particular praise, since there is a clear example of dancing to song in Campion's *The Lords' Masque*, with the ditty suited to the device (happy reference being made to the royal bride and groom). It is headed "A song and dance triumphant of the Masquers", and begins, "Dance,

dance! and visit now the shadows of our joy".
Campion, it needs to recall, was quite as much
musician as poet, and was in the habit of composing
vocal music for his own masques. In his *Masque for
Lord Haddington's Marriage*, in 1608, a quire of six
occupied an elevated position and sang to broken
music. Accordingly, it would seem that it was to
Campion's method Bacon was referring, though it
should be borne in mind that in *The Masque of
Mountebanks*, a Gray's Inn masque of 1618, with
whose production Bacon was doubtless associated,
there was a "song and dance together", the words
beginning "Frolick measures now become you".

Bacon is careful to distinguish between "dancing
to song" and "dancing in song", but the two are
not likely to be confused if we bear in mind that the
masquers proper neither spoke nor sang. In Bacon's
day, none save the professional players engaged for
the anti-masques indulged in song and dance. The
combination savoured too much of the ribald
theatre jig and was to him abomination:

Acting in song, especially in dialogues, hath an
extreme good grace; I say acting, not dancing (for that
is a mean and vulgar thing); and the voices of the
dialogue would be strong and manly (a base and a
tenor, no treble) and the ditty high and tragical, not
nice or dainty. Several quires placed one over against

another, and taking the voice by catches, anthem-wise, give great pleasure.

There is here condemnation of Jonson's *The Gipsies Metamorphosed*, which, as given no fewer than three times before the King at different places in 1621, had at least one racy song and dance. The vulgarity of this summer masque is beyond all question. Bacon's reference to dialogues in song is apt to switch the minds of those who are well versed in the history of the masque on to the wrong track and to set them thinking of recitative, since recitative had been experimented with by Nicholas Lanier in *The Vision of Delight* and *Lovers Made Men*; but the new Italian scheme met with no favour, and Bacon ignores the innovation. A dialogue song was either a song in which the lines were sung alternately by two or more voices, as in the song of the four pages in *The Masque of Mountebanks*, or a song openly given and responded to at intervals by a seen or unseen chorus. Thus Campion calls "Breathe you now, while Io Hymen" in *The Lords' Masque* a dialogue song, though it has no conversational quality. An example of the kind of dialogue song commended by Bacon occurs, curiously enough, in the opening scene of Chapman's *Masque of the Middle Temple and Lincoln's Inn*, where the priests worship the sun in song to lute accompaniment and are "answered by voices and instruments from the Temple and from other parts of the Hall".[1]

In his zeal to make a case, Dowden strives to show that Bacon's reference to "double masques" was inspired by Beaumont's masque, but all he succeeds in demonstrating is his own ignorance of the meaning of the term. Contrary to his opinion, the term had nothing whatever to do with anti-masques, and has no application to Beaumont's masque. Recall what Bacon writes:

Double masques, one of men, another of ladies, addeth state and variety; but all is nothing, except the room be kept neat and clean.

The double masque was an old device, long in vogue before Jonson established the principle of the anti-masque, but it was never more than occasionally adopted. Court examples are to be traced in the Revels Accounts so far back as the period of 1570. Normally the masquers were all of a sex, generally men (though in Queen's masques they were commonly women); but in double masques there were two sets, a male and a female, and the sets, after entering and dancing separately, finally intermingled. A typical double masque was Jonson's *Masque of Hymen*, the book of which clearly reveals

[1] See Foscarini's letter in the *Calendar of State Papers, Venetian*, 1610–13, p. 532.

PLATE V

A Courtly Maſque:

The Deuice called, The VVorld toſt at Tennı

As it hath beene diuers times Preſented to the
Contentment of many Noble and Worthy
Spectators:

By the PRINCE *his Seruants.*

Inuented and ſet
downe, By } Tho: *Middleton*
&
William Rowley } Gent

Title-page of the public masque, *The World Tost at Tennis*,
as acted by the Prince's Men in 1620

the system pursued. It is notable that the last of the order was likewise the last of the great Caroline masques, Davenant's *Salmacida Spolia*, a production of superb pictorial beauty made in 1640, in which the male masquers were headed by the King and the female by the Queen.

It is much to be doubted if Inns of Court masques were ever double masques. Nothing of the kind is on record. On this score, Dowden is hoist with his own petard. Oddly enough, while Beaumont's masque was not, as argued, of the double order, Campion's *The Lords' Masque* came within the category. Indeed, if any partiality is shown in Bacon's essay, it is for the work—or perhaps one should say the methods of presenting the work— of the innovative poet-musician. Here, for once, friendship and cold judgment joined hands. Let it not be forgotten that Campion had collaborated with Francis Davison in writing *The Masque of Proteus*, that transitional spectacle which the members of Gray's Inn presented at Court in the Shrovetide of 1594, and in so doing pioneered the way for the graceful pictorial fantasies of Ben Jonson and Inigo Jones.

Chapter XI

THE WEDDING OF POETRY
AND SONG

Most cultured people to-day agree with Théophile
Gautier that the words that are usually sung are not
otherwise worth listening to; but there was a time
when real poets wrote lyrics and were not always
content that their muse should be the mere hand-
maiden to Euterpe. On this point, however, information is exasperatingly obscure. We do not
know whether, in Elizabethan days, when a brand-
new song was first sung socially, it was the custom
for the words first to be recited that the assembly
might fully savour the lyrist's quality, or whether
the practice, so far as it was observed, was wholly
confined to the theatre. All we know for certain is
that the thing was done in Ben Jonson's *Cynthia's
Revels*, when that fine-drawn Court satire was produced at the Blackfriars in 1601. In the fourth act of
the play, Hedon sings "The Kiss", a song of his own
composition, and Amorphous, in the same breath
that he commends it, maintains that he had written
and composed a better one. Having "the note and

ditty" with him, he proposes reading the song to the ladies, and begins by explaining the circumstances which inspired it. He then recites his "Ode to the Glove", and, after some entreaty (that eternal drawing-room routine) sings it to Hedon's musical accompaniment.

It may be that here Jonson is simply mirroring social habit, but on that score history is painfully silent.[1] The curious thing to note, however, is that,

---

[1] There is, however, one slender item of evidence which lends colour to the supposition that the practice of reciting a lyric before singing it originated socially. On November 17, 1590, a Triumph at Tilt was held at Westminster in celebration of the Queen's birthday. At the close of the account given of the proceedings by Sir William Segar in his *Honor Military and Civil*, Bk. III, chap. 54 (1602), we are told that: "Her Majesty beholding these armed knights coming towards her, did suddenly hear a music so sweet and secret, as everyone thereat greatly marvelled. And harkening to that excellent melody, the earth as it were opening, there appeared a pavilion...like unto the sacred temple of the Virgins Vestal....The music aforesaid was accompanied with these verses, pronounced and sung by M. Hales her Majesty's servant, a gentleman in that art excellent, and for his voice both commendable and admirable". Then follows the famous lyric of three sextets, "My golden locks time hath to silver turned", generally attributed to Peele. It seems highly probable that this was really the work of Sir Henry Lee, who had long superintended these birthday tournaments and was known to be making his last appearance in festivals of the sort. Hitherto, it has been assumed by Sir Edmund Chambers and others that by "pronounced and sung" Segar merely meant to say somewhat tautologically that Robert Hales the lutenist did no more than vocalise the poem, but, if we take his phrasing literally, as we are certainly entitled to do, it would point to a practice of recitation before song.

while the proportion of songs given on the stage in new plays from this time on which were read aloud before being sung was singularly small, yet the practice was carried on intermittently until the middle of the eighteenth century. Allowing that there was a pre-existent, well-established social custom of the sort, its stage use, even at an early period, was not in all cases a matter of simple realism. Realism could hardly have been the inspiring cause of the procedure in the second act of Middleton's comedy, *Blurt Master Constable* (produced, it is to be noted, much about the same time as *Cynthia's Revels*), where Imperia, when alone with her two maids, says: "Ho, prithee, sing! stay, stay; here's Hippolito's sonnet; first read it and then sing it". As example after example crops up, puzzlement climbs on the back of puzzlement. No sooner has one arrived at the conclusion that it was deemed requisite that the audience should first savour the verse, lest its quality and import should be marred in the singing, than hard fact advances blunt contradiction. None of the songs in Jonson's *Poetaster*, which immediately followed, was read out before being sung. And how are we to account for the ceremony observed in the fourth act of Field's *Amends for Ladies*, a Whitefriars comedy of early Jacobean days? Subtle, accompanied by his page, and bearing a paper, arrives at daybreak before Lady Bright's house. After reading out a poem of two stanzas invoking the appearance of his goddess, he bids the page sing the lines; but all to no purpose—despite this double appeal, no lady emerges.

Pioneer of the stage practice, Jonson was also the first to utilise it in reverse. In the third act of *The Devil is an Ass*, a play of his later maturity, Wittipol hands his friend Manly a poem in praise of Mrs Fitzdottrell, written by him to an air familiar to Manly, and asks him to sing it. Manly complies, but on the charmer's appearance at a window, discreetly departs, leaving Wittipol and the lady alone. At the end of the scene of courtship which ensues, Wittipol, as if to demonstrate that the words of the song were his own personal tribute to her beauty, repeats them, and is overheard by her husband. Here the arrangement is so clumsy that it gives one the impression that rare old Ben was enamoured of his own poem. Two years later, after having rung the changes on the idea that he had first exploited, Jonson returned to his first principles, not in a play, however, but in a Court masque. In *Pleasure Reconciled to Virtue*, as represented at Whitehall early in 1618, the last song is first recited by Mercury and then sung by five soloists and a chorus.

If we can safely assume that social custom really inspired the preliminary reading of stage song in our early drama, the chances are that the main characteristics of that custom were faithfully reflected in the scene in Brome's Caroline comedy, *The Novella*, wherein Horatio presents his tribute of verse, together with the music to which it had been set, to Victoria. "Please you to read 'em, sir", says the lady, "and in requital of such a debt, my maid shall sing 'hem for you." Here, Jacconetta, the maid, opportunely enters, and her mistress bids her "observe the ditty". Horatio then reads the whole three stanzas of his song, and Jacconetta, having the then not uncommon accomplishment of reading music at sight, at once sings them.

But there were no hard and fast rules for the employment of the stage convention, and it was certainly not social habit that was reflected by Shirley when he pressed it into service—not without rhyme, but certainly without reason—in his *Love in a Maze*. In the fourth act of the comedy, Gerald is alone in his room and full of melancholy. In answer to his inquiry, his page informs him that a lyric he had written and sent to a musician to be set to music had come back completed. He then bids the boy "first read it", adding, "'tis yet no song, infuse a soul into it". The page obeys, though why he should have been asked to read out a poem when nobody but its author was present to hear it is difficult to divine. True, the thing might have been done for the better satisfaction of the audience, but in that case Gerald set a very bad example, seeing that no sooner had he heard the song than he went to sleep.

One point at least can be determined. If, in the beginning, this curious old stage practice obtained its right of existence from social custom, it is fairly certain that it long outlasted what had inspired it. It may be, however, that in Restoration days it still had some basis in actuality, such as entitled Etherege to make employment of it. In the fourth act of his *The Man of Mode*, Sir Fopling Flutter confesses he has written a song in praise of Mrs Loveit, and, handing the sheet to young Bellair, begs him to read it to the company. Then, by general request, though not without many protestations about the state of his voice, etc., etc., Sir Fopling carols the ditty. But, viewing the choppings and changings of fashion, it comes with something of a surprise to find Steele, some forty years later, resorting twice to the old practice. There is a scene in the second act of *The Funeral* which passes in Lord Brumpton's house, and in this Mrs Fardingale enters to two ladies and conveys the information that she purposes entertaining them with a new song fresh from the mint, written by her cousin Campley, and "set to a pretty air". Lady Sharlot reaches for the scroll of verse, and, a little before Campley himself comes on the scene, reads the lines aloud. Then Mrs Fardingale calls for her lute, and, having persuaded the luckless poet to hold the music sheet on his hat, proceeds to do the luckless song to death in a sequence of spasmodic squalls.

Steele's second example is much less happy. It occurs at the opening of the second act of *The Lying Lover*, in the scene of Penelope's lodgings. Lettice, Penelope's maid, reminds her that she has not yet heard the song written about her by her languishing lover; and the lady, taking the proffered paper, nonchalantly reads out the lines, "To Celia's Spirit". Then, all of a sudden, we find ourselves in the old outmoded theatre, and highly offended by the stench of the candles. It would appear that neither of the actresses representing the mistress and the maid could sing, for Penelope recalls that her music master awaits her in another room, and sends for him. But as he fails to materialise, and the ensuing stage direction merely says "here the song is performed to a spinet", it would seem that the song was most unillusively rendered behind the scenes, while the women listened.

Even in 1720, after the passing of wellnigh a

century and a quarter, the old convention was still persisting. In *The Refusal* of Colley Cibber, there is, in the fourth act, a delicious satire on the fashionable "musick-meetings" of the period. Witling, the vacuous author-composer of a new cantata, is not only cajoled into reciting his own "poem", so that the assembly may indulge in sarcastic comments of a wide application, but yields to the demands for the vocalisation of his lines, and puts a severe strain upon the reserve which politeness dictates by singing the whole in a woolly and wobbling falsetto.

As one reads in the old play one hears the faint rumbling of the mills of the gods. Time came when in a not unsimilar scene Cibber was himself satirised. In Fielding's *Historical Register for the year* 1736 (an amusing *revue*, in the French sense of the abused term, produced at the Haymarket in 1737), Medley, by request, in the opening scene, reads out his "singing prologue" called "Ode to the New Year", a satire on Cibber, the poet laureate's birthday and other regulation Court odes, after which a number of vocalists come on and sing it. Sourwit's request to the author is significant, inasmuch as it probably hints at the real reason why the old convention was still to some extent maintained. "Dear Medley", he says, "let me hear you read it; possibly it may

be sung so fine, I may not understand a word of
it."

It is a nice question how long this time-worn
principle of "first read, then sing" received exemplification. All one can say for certain is that it was
still to the fore after George III came to the throne.
The last example that has swum into my ken occurs
in the opening scene of Charles Macklin's comedy,
The True-Born Irishman, a mordant piece of Sinn
Fein propaganda written long before Sinn Fein became a shibboleth, produced in Dublin at the Crow
Street Theatre in 1762 and afterwards unsuccessfully
acted in London as *The Irish Fine Lady*. When the
play opens we are in Murrogh O'Dogherty's house.
In the course of the action Count Mushroom reads
his "Extempore on the famous Mrs Diggerty's
dancing at court", nine lines of anaemic verse, and,
after having periphrastically conveyed to the
company that the effusion had been melodised by
Dr Arne, begs Mrs Diggerty (alias O'Dogherty)
to honour him by singing it. After the usual protestations about the state of her voice, the lady
consents, taking care as a preliminary to go carefully
over her "sol-la-mi-fa-sol".

Chapter XII

THE SECRET OF THE "BAD QUARTOS"

In an age when specialisation is growing more and more a ruling principle in all kinds of activities, it will probably be futile to speak of its dangers; yet it is essential for scholars to grasp that specialisation in matters of Elizabethan inquiry brings with it as much bane as blessing. Though a great writer may have risen superior to his environment, his work inevitably bears the seal of his hour upon it, and the better we comprehend the form and pressure of that hour, the more likely we are to adjudge of his mission and make allowance for his shortcomings. There is little need to labour the point that all scrutiny of Shakespeare in a vacuum leads to a sad distortion of the truth. No one, for example, who is soundly versed in the theatrical conditions and stage history of the last quarter of the sixteenth century and the first quarter of the seventeenth could give a moment's entertainment to the idea that Shakespeare's plays were the work of anybody save a journeyman dramatist. Belief to the contrary springs from ill-

thinking and half-knowledge, only to be fostered
by popular ignorance which sees a mystery where
there is none. Mordant as are these reflections, they
bear application in a modified sense to the existing
attitude towards what are known among Elizabethan scholars as the "Bad Quartos". Scholarship
still labours under the delusion that all that is
humanly possible has been done when each of these
sophistications has been segregated and given careful
examination under the microscope without thought
of its possible kinship to the others, though the only
material outcome of this procedure has been a
welter of confusing theories, most of them mere-
tricious and unsatisfying. What really requires to be
undertaken is associative inquiry, and that too with
some considerable widening of the purview. I am
thoroughly convinced that the truth will emerge
when we examine collectively, seeking in all for
characteristics in common, not only the four quasi-
Shakespearian quartos which, following Mr A. W.
Pollard's lead, are now usually styled "bad", but
also two earlier quartos which, there is good reason
to believe, are piracies of Shakespeare's work, and
any other abbreviated plays whose originals are extant and which may be safely taken as surreptitious.

Need of extensive collation of this order is indicated by the fact that, notwithstanding all the

theories of origin which scholars have advanced—
some of them highly complex and most ingenious—
no one theory has been hit upon which accounts
for all the distinguishing characteristics of the "Bad
Quartos". In the beginning play was made with an
unaided stenographer, but in process of time it
became apparent that the services of this worthy
were inadequate to meet all the requirements, and,
not finding it in their hearts wholly to discard him,
investigators bestowed upon him the aid and comfort of a hypothetical player, otherwise a miserable
puppet worked by many strings, one accommodat-
ing enough for a trifle to sink his loyalty to his fellows, and inconsistent enough in his mental make-
up to have now quite astonishing mnemonic powers
and now the most wretched of memories, according
to the needs of the manipulator. Remarkably
enough, however, not even the most elaborate
hypothesis of the maturer order suffices to explain
why in all the "Bad Quartos" certain scenes are
omitted or occur out of their proper order, or why
speeches, in whole or part, have been frequently
transposed. Save when dealing with the spurious
Hamlet quarto (and then only in connexion with the
transposition of scenes), investigators have remained
significantly silent about these points. If it had only
struck them that the same peculiarities were

observable in other abbreviated plays of the Elizabethan period, what a quantity of idle theorising
might have been stayed!

Once we see that all these piracies have differentiae
in common, some glimmering of a broad system of
manufacture becomes apparent, and what we have
to do is to determine what were the necessities which
created that system and to approximate the period
when it was first put in practice. Doubtless I shall
be accused of flagrantly begging the question in
styling all abbreviated Elizabethan plays piracies,
seeing that it has been maintained by eminent
scholars who ought really to have known better that
certain of these shortened versions were made by the
players possessing the full texts for their own particular use while travelling about the country. There
is not, however, a scintilla of evidence in favour of
this assumption; and, even if I could be brought to
believe that reputable London players ruthlessly
maltreated their plays for country performance, I
could never concede that, while the plays still
remained active in their repertory, they would have
disposed of such libels on their good taste and
intelligence to the press. Recall, furthermore, their
general attitude towards publication. Heywood, as
actor-dramatist, is surely an authority on this point,
and Heywood once wrote concerning plays that the

players thought it "against their peculiar profit to have them come into print". If this was true of the genuine, how much more so of the spurious? Assuming that abbreviated versions were regularly made by the London players for country performance, and that these could, by common consent, be given without much delay to the press, how comes it that publications of the sort ceased early in James's reign? Are we not entitled to conclude that these versions were surreptitious, and that the owners of the originals found means of preventing them from getting into print? It is only by postulating that they were made for some of the regular country companies of a certain respectability that we can account at once for their distinguishing characteristics and their early publication.

Though play-piracy may have begun earlier and lasted longer, the evidence as we have it warrants us only to conclude that a certain slapdash method of appropriation existed from 1592 to 1603, or thereabouts. Unless I greatly mistake, an absurdly simple hypothesis reads all the riddles set by these stolen versions. However obtained, it was essential that the adapter should have a fairly sound copy of the full acting text before him when he began his work. We need not assume that he had any great literary capacity, but it is incumbent upon us to conclude that he was well versed in the plays of his time and had a full knowledge of the quality and limitations of the company for which he was about to labour. Aware that that company was made up of, say, a dozen players—and the best of regular country companies in Elizabeth's reign rarely had more— his first task would be to go over the manuscript and see how many of the *dramatis personae* could be safely eliminated. Sometimes, as in the making of the spurious versions of *Romeo and Juliet* and *Hamlet*, few or none could be spared, and sometimes, as in the piracy of *Henry V*, there would be wholesale slaughter of the innocents. Next came the casting of the characters. Doubling was then a common practice in both town and country (it often meant trebling), and a sliding scale of doubling would have to be followed, according to the size of the company and the number of characters left standing. The adapter avoided it as much as possible, because, since doubled characters never met, the more he resorted to it the greater difficulty he encountered in preparing the text. It was principally doubling that led to the transposition and (less frequently) the elimination of scenes. Now and again it occasioned a speech to be pared, sometimes a difficult task because when a declaration of some importance was deleted, the adapter had to arrange for its utterance elsewhere.

PLATE VI

A N
EXCELLENT
conceited Tragedie
O F
Romeo and Iuliet.

As it hath been often (with great applaufe)
plaid publiquely, by the right Ho-
nourable the L. of *Hanfdon*
his Seruants.

LONDON,
Printed by Iohn Danter.
1 5 9 7

Title-page of the spurious quarto of *Romeo and Juliet*, 1597

Apart from these necessities, there was abbreviation for its own sake. Long reflective soliloquies were cut to the bone: evidently they had no appeal to the rural mind. There may or may not have been a time limit for country performance: it cannot be predicated. Abbreviated plays varied in length from the 1465 lines of *Orlando Furioso* to the 2143 lines of *Hamlet*. The average country play was undoubtedly short commons, but, in the period under discussion and perhaps later, we may be sure that the performance was eked out by the giving of one of those short highly popular musical farces of a ribald order known as "jigs", which, to an audience familiar with May-games (to which the jig is supposed to have owed its origin), would have irresistible appeal.

Eager as I am to proceed to demonstration of the results of this complex procedure on the part of the adapter by citation from representative examples of his work, I am given pause by the necessity to consider the nature of the copy on which he based. It will be recalled that, when ushering in the First Folio, Heminge and Condell claimed, and claimed unduly, that "as where (before) you were abus'd with diverse stolne and surreptitious copies, maimed and deformed by the frauds and stealthes of injurious impostors, that expos'd them: even those are now

offer'd to your view cur'd, and perfect of their
limbes, and all the rest, absolute in their numbers,
as he conceiv'd them". There is here no absolute
implication of resort to stenography, nor does the
phrasing exclude its use, but since stenography was
certainly brought into play by the pirates on occasion, it is essential to point out that shorthand writing
of any particular competency could hardly be held
accountable for all the maimings and deformities in
the "Bad Quartos", and that there is surely reference
to the purposeful eliminations and transpositions to
be noted in those texts. Improbable almost to the
verge of impossibility as it sounds, I am compelled
by the logic of the situation to conclude that in most
cases the adapter had access to the prompt copy.
Not otherwise can we account for the curious
identity of passages in a piracy and its prototype,
passages not only having the same wording, but
the same capitalisation, the same italicisation and
the same punctuation. Seeing that the piracy was
always the first to get into print, coincidences of
the sort are truly remarkable.

The abbreviated texts which I have examined
conjunctively, and purpose discussing with necessary brevity, are *The First Part of the Contention* of
1594, *The True Tragedie of Richard Duke of Yorke* of
1595, the *Orlando Furioso* quarto of 1594, and the

four "Bad Quartos". In the case of the first two, I
agree with Mr Peter Alexander, without endorsing
all his arguments, that so far from being the originals
from which Shakespeare derived 2 and 3 *Henry VI*,
the exact reverse is the case, and believe that they
were pirated versions made for country acting, and,
most probably, for the one country company. The
older theory fails to solve all the problems they
present, and they have all the distinguishing characteristics observable in the "Bad Quartos". In the
course of his initial discussion of the subject,[1] Mr
Alexander quotes from a speech of Warwick's in
The Contention:

> Then Yorke aduise thy selfe and take thy time,
> Claime thou the Crowne, and set thy standard vp,
> And in the same aduance the milk-white Rose,
> And then to gard it, will I rouse the Beare,
> Inuiron'd with ten thousand Ragged-staues
> To aide and helpe thee for to win thy right.

"This nonsense", he adds, "made up of reminiscences of York's speech in act I, sc. I, and from act V,
sc. I, was put down by the reporter to fill a gap at
the end of act II, sc. 2." One hardly sees why this
should be styled an act of reminiscence, seeing that
Mr Alexander is forced to conclude on the general

[1] See his article "2 *Henry VI* and the copy for *The Contention*"
in *The Times Literary Supplement* of October 9, 1924.

evidence that "the reporter" had an abbreviated copy of the play before him. If abbreviated, whence was it obtained? To my mind, this conglomerate and other features of the piracy indicate that the adapter had access to the full text. Not being able to go the whole hog and venture this opinion, Mr Alexander is compelled to assume the assistance of two of the original players simply because some of the speeches are fully and correctly given. In support of this view, he draws attention to a sound transcription of two sequential speeches which have been transposed from act IV, sc. 5, an act of faithfulness which is better accounted for by access to the original than in any other way. That idea acquires further cogency when we find a long stage direction from act II, sc. 3, given *verbatim et literatim* in the piracy. Here Mr Alexander admits a manuscript source, but having committed himself to the regulation "reporter" hypothesis, he is forced in the end to confess that "this combination of reporter and transcript presents further and more difficult problems to the student of the text". In other words, the assumption creates as many difficulties as it solves.

As for *The True Tragedie of Richard Duke of Yorke*, it is surprising how long the truth about it has been delayed. Most indubitably, it is an abridgment of 3 *Henry VI*. In his second paper dealing with the

"Contention" plays,[1] Mr Alexander clearly shows by apt juxtaposing of certain passages how the quarto mangles and perverts the Shakespearian text. But he is positive that these corruptions "cannot be attributed to a compositor, or transcriber, or abridger, or to their combined efforts", and in support of his belief falls back on the contentions of Dr W. W. Greg, as advanced by him in his redaction of *Orlando Furioso*, published in the Malone Society series. While maintaining that the sole version of Greene's play that has come down to us consists for the most part of reported matter, Dr Greg finds it necessary to account for what appears to him capricious transposing and the confusion of lines, and once more summons to his aid his own original theory of an assistant actor's defective memory. How blunderers of this sort gained any employment in the Elizabethan theatre it would be difficult to say; yet, if we are to believe present-day investigators, every framer of the pirated version of a play had at least one of them at his beck. There is quite too much method in the old adapter's madness for it to have been inspired time after time in this fortuitous way. That the concocter of *The True Tragedie* had something better to rely upon than the

[1] "3 *Henry VI* and *Richard Duke of York*" in *The Times Literary Supplement* for November 13, 1924.

aid and counsel of an uncertain-minded player is demonstrated by the fact that, with all its faults, it gives a sounder version of certain Shakespearian passages than the Folio copy of the original. Once again one has to postulate access to an authentic manuscript. It is Mr Alexander's belief that the two players who acted Warwick and Clifford in 2 *Henry VI* assisted the adapter in the making of *The Contention* and *The True Tragedie*. With that I wholly disagree, but I think we may safely assume that both piracies were devised by the one man for the one company of country players. There is no reason to believe that surreptitious versions were made at any other period except when their originals were in the first blush of their success; and at that time there would be little excuse for defective memories, and none at all for players capable of sustaining important characters like Warwick and Clifford. One could understand the calling in of members of the original cast if the aim were at a full and accurate text, but the facts are otherwise: *The True Tragedie* is a third short in length of the Folio play. The *Henry VI* trilogy dates, inceptively, from March 1592; *The Contention* was registered in March 1594; and *The True Tragedie* published in 1595. There were country companies of some little capacity at the time when the two piracies must have

been made, and, since their profits were not sufficiently large to enable them to purchase new plays,
they must have relied to a considerable extent on
procuring surreptitious copies of novelties. Despite
the fact that they made occasional appearances in
London, Sussex's Men were of this order, and were
granted a special country licence in April 1593.
Whether or not the play was illegitimately obtained, there is some significance in the circumstance
that *George a Greene*, which dates from 1593 and was
published as acted by this company in 1599, exists
only in abbreviated form. Coincidences are often
coincidences and nothing more; yet, nevertheless, it
is curious that Sussex's Men returned to London in
December 1593, and acted at the Rose until February
6 following, and that exactly a month later *The
Contention* was entered on the Stationers' books.

Taking the collated piracies in the order of
publication, I find that something more needs to be
said of *Orlando Furioso*, the only extant version of
which was published in 1594, without mention of
the acting company but with the insinuation that
the text represented the play as it had been acted at
Court—an oblique mendacity. This title-page equivocation is *prima facie* evidence of a rank spuriousness
which the testimony of the text fully establishes. In
discussing the peculiarities of the quarto in his *Two*

Elizabethan Stage Abridgements, Dr W. W. Greg clearly reveals that it is a piratical version of Greene's play made for country performance, though he denies the piracy and concludes that it was devised by the play's original owners for their own country use. It needs the summoning of some extra moral courage to differ from so brilliant a scholar, but here I must perforce call up my reserves. Let me first admit that the salient characteristics of the play as we have it are defined with admirable terseness by Dr Greg:

> The text of *Orlando Furioso* printed in 1594 proves on examination to be a version severely abridged by the excision of scenes, speeches and passages of dialogue, as well as by compression and omission of characters, for performance by a reduced cast in a strictly limited time. Further than this the version has been adapted, by the insertion of episodes of rough clownage and horseplay, to the tastes of a lower class of audience, and there may perhaps have been some intentional vulgarization of the language throughout.

We are also told that in the making of the text a double process went on, that there was expansion as well as deletion, about a hundred lines having been added. Yet the whole comprises only 1465 lines, or some 800 lines short of the average play of the time. To my mind, what especially equates the play with unmistakable piracies is the tearing away of sundry passages from their contexts and the planting of them elsewhere. Dr Greg is fully alive to this peculiarity without seeing in it any significance, and cites as an example the mock-Angelica episode in ll. 1058-66, where one line of the addition— "Where's your sweet hart Medor?"—has been transferred from a passage elsewhere deleted. Wholly averse as he is from entertaining the possibility that the adapter had access to the original prompt-book, he finds difficulty in countering evidence indicative of that access. To begin with, he is unable to account for the fact that in 1, 2, ll. 378-9, the name of the Countie Rossilion appears in a stage direction at the head of the scene, though no such character is to be found in the play. Let the character have been eliminated when it may, this, of a surety, was an error of transcription, due to mechanical copying. Again, Dr Greg is puzzled to know how the adapter got the names of Melissa, Namus and Turpin, since none of them is mentioned in the text of the quarto. Here also, I think, we have proof of access to a manuscript of some sort. Then, again, we have to account for the fact that the two roundelays used by Sacripant to delude Orlando are, as Dr Greg says, "practically letter-perfect"; a very remarkable thing, seeing that they are not included in Edward Alleyn's part of Orlando, now preserved at Dulwich

College. One cannot get away from the conclusion that the adapter, having somehow got access to the prompt copy, was enabled also to copy the actual stage scrolls bearing the roundelays. (Letters and cognate things were always then written out in full.) But Dr Greg will have none of this, and argues with no great plausibility that the abbreviated version was made by a company which possessed the properties of the play but had neither the prompt copy nor the players' parts. It seems to me, however, that to repudiate a manuscript basis for the text is to leave the problem hanging in the air.

Next we come to the bad quarto of *Romeo and Juliet* issued by John Danter in 1597. Here we have an abbreviated text, some 800 lines shorter than the authentic quarto of 1599, but with no character omitted and no scene wholly unrepresented. Unless the piratical company for whom it was made numbered considerably over a dozen—an unlikely contingency—there must have been much doubling in the performance. Transposition of phrases, that common feature in all surreptitious copies, now and again occurs. For example, in the dance scene in act I, sc. 5, Capulet has a speech ending with:

I promise you but for your company
I would haue bin a bed an houre agoe:
Light to my chamber hoe.

PLATE VII

A
Moſt pleaſaunt and
excellent conceited Co-
medie, of Syr *Iohn Falſtaffe*, and the
merrie Wiues of *Windſor*.

Entermixed with ſundrie
variable and pleaſing humors, of Syr *Hugh*
the Welch Knight, Iuſtice *Shallow*, and his
wiſe Couſin M. *Slender*.

With the ſwaggering vaine of Auncient
Piſtoll, and Corporall *Nym*.

By *William Shakeſpeare*.

As it hath bene diuers times Acted by the right Honorable
my Lord Chamberlaines ſeruants. Both before her
Maieſtie, and elſe-where.

LONDON
Printed by T. C. for Arthur Iohnſon, and are to be ſold at
his ſhop in Powles Church-yard, at the ſigne of the
Flower de Leuſe and the Crowne.
1602.

Title-page of the spurious quarto of *The Merry Wives
of Windsor*, 1602

These lines are not to be found in the corresponding speech in Q. 2, where, however, there is a similar leave-taking, but in the received text they occur at act III, sc. 4, ll. 6, 7, 34. In one of their careful studies of "the stolne and surreptitious texts" published in *The Times Literary Supplement* for August 14, 1919, Professor J. Dover Wilson and Mr A. W. Pollard discuss this passage and maintain that the player of Capulet lent assistance to the adapter; but it hardly seems credible that the player of a part would end one speech with the tag of another, even when the circumstances were identical. There are too many analogues in other piracies for the thing to have been done otherwise than deliberately.

When we turn to the spurious *Henry V* of 1600 we find ourselves confronted by a version in which there has been a serious reduction of the *dramatis personae*, as well as a good deal of textual condensation. Some scenes certainly have been omitted, but we cannot be sure that all the scenes specified by Daniel in his introduction to the parallel texts of the play as unrepresented should be included in this category, seeing that there is good reason to believe that later expansion of the text (with the addition of at least one scene) took place. Daniel comments on the identity of the curious spelling of simple words in the bad quartos of *Henry V* and *The Merry*

Wives of Windsor, and thinks that this was due to the printer, Thomas Creede, having printed both. But it is equally likely to have been due to the adapter, a possibility which suggests that both texts were prepared by the one man for the one company. Daniel also draws attention to the fact that the two scenes in the French camp in Shakespeare's *Henry V* are represented in the piracy only by the first, and that that scene is finished off with the tag to the second, a curious transference somewhat similar to the one already cited from the spurious *Romeo and Juliet*, which, as he says, "brings in the sun at midnight".

It cannot be too strongly emphasised that these transpositions of scenes and passages form the prime denotement of the Elizabethan play-pirate.[1] There was undoubtedly a regular system of manufacture, born of the particular needs, but, unless we are to conclude that all the surreptitious copies made in the last decade of the sixteenth century were the work of one man,[2] it is curious that it should have

---

[1] For a curious example of transposition in *The Taming of a Shrew* indicating that Shakespeare's *Taming of the Shrew* was the original, see the recent Cambridge recension of the Shakespearian play (1928), Professor Dover Wilson's notes, p. 149, ll. 10–18.

[2] Which would be a sheer flouting of the evidence. The spurious *Hamlet* and *Merry Wives* texts were not made by the one hand. The compiler of the latter is partial to the solecism, "exit omnes", of which no example is to be found in the former.

been an open secret. Little wonder that piecemeal
investigation has been so poor in results. Transpositions are to be found in abundance in the bad
quarto of *The Merry Wives*, published in 1602, a
careful reprint of which, edited with notes by Dr
Greg, has been issued in the useful Tudor and
Stuart Library series by the Clarendon Press. A few
examples will probably now suffice. Lines 81–6 in
the quarto occur later in the folio, at III, 4, 63, a
scene omitted in the piracy. Similarly, ll. 129–30 of
the second scene of the quarto are to be found at I,
1. 273 of the Folio, a portion otherwise ignored by
the adapter. Then, again, sc. 3, ll. 164–7, is composed
of two transpositions. Sc. 4 is abbreviated, and
summarises, with transpositions, the Folio text at
I, 4, 1–131. Moreover, some lines in this scene are
taken from various other parts of the Shakespearian
play.[1]

Though none of the "Bad Quartos" has been half
so much discussed as the *Hamlet* quarto, most of what
has been written about it is the mere spoiling of good
paper. This is not surprising when we come to
consider how long scholars laboured under the
delusion that it presented the text of Shakespeare's

---

[1] Extreme caution must be exercised in collating the two texts,
because the Folio text is not the full original text, but a revision of
it.

"first sketch" of the play (it is still occasionally acted as such: a left-handed compliment to the supreme dramatist). What we require to recognise now is that it is only by taking it as a link in the general evidence revealing the method of making surreptitious copies that we can arrive at the full truth concerning it. There is no need, I trust, for me to recapitulate here the arguments formerly advanced by me with the aim of demonstrating that the spurious *Hamlet* quarto was printed from a prompt copy prepared for the use of a country company.[1] Little more remains to be done beyond stressing the remarkable transpositions of scenes and passages in the piracy. Largely due to the early misconception regarding the origin of the text, the scent of a red herring has been drawn across the trail by the contention that the arrangement of the scenes brings about a closer knitting of the action than is to be found in the genuine texts. That there are two opinions on this point becomes apparent after a perusal of Dr B. A. P. Van Dam's *The Text of Shakespeare's "Hamlet"*, wherein the matter is fully discussed. Whatever betterment, however, has been made, there is no reason to conclude that it was

---

[1] See the paper on "The mystery of the Hamlet First Quarto" in my *Shakespeare's Workshop*. Also the article on "The pirates of Hamlet" in *The Criterion* for July 1929.

PLATE VIII

THE
Tragicall Historie of
HAMLET

Prince of Denmarke

By William Shake-speare.

As it hath beene diuerse times acted by his Highnesse seruants in the Cittie of London : as also in the two V-
niuersities of Cambridge and Oxford, and else-where

At London printed for N:L. and Iohn Trundell.
1603,

Title-page of the spurious quarto of *Hamlet*, 1603

arrived at otherwise than accidentally. In Elizabethan days it was customary for the plot to amble
along at a jog-trot with occasional haltings by the
way; and nothing warrants us in believing that
neat construction was looked upon as a prime
desideratum. The idea that a play-pirate would have
given himself a lot of extra trouble on that score is
too preposterous for a moment's consideration.
Something more exigent (possibly the casting of
characters for doubling) must have brought about
the rearrangement. Moreover, there is not alone the
shuffling of the scenes to be accounted for, but likewise the transposition of divers passages. Of the
latter I need cite no examples here, since the reader
will find the whole of them discussed by Dr Van
Dam in the chapter of his book already referred to.
Dr Van Dam's theory is that these brief transpositions were due to the blundering of incompetent
actors, the text having been taken down in the
theatre exactly as it was uttered. But this hypothesis
often fails to apply. As a case in point, why should
Hamlet in the closet scene appropriate two lines
(ll. 1475-6) from an earlier speech made by his
father's ghost (I, 5, 49-50)?—

Whose heart went hand in hand euen with that vow,
He made to you in marriage.

It would be idle to proffer here in explanation that the one actor had a sudden recollection of words uttered by the other at a moment when his memory had betrayed him, for, on turning to the ghost's speech as given in the spurious quarto, we find that it omits the lines which Hamlet borrows. Surely, there could be no clearer example of deliberate transference. But, puzzle over the matter as one may, it seems impossible to determine why, in most piracies, snippets of this trivial order should have been systematically juggled with. However, in spite of that impasse, I make bold to claim that the problem of the "Bad Quartos", as well as of abbreviated plays in general, has now been solved.

Chapter XIII

DOUBLE TITLES IN ELIZABETHAN DRAMA

Among the many interesting features presented by a recent important book on *The Plays of Beaumont and Fletcher* by Mr E. H. C. Oliphant—a valiant attempt to determine the chronology of all the plays in which the two dramatists had a hand, and to assign to each his individual work—is a theory concerning the origin and significance of the double title in early drama which demands the fullest consideration. There is a growing feeling that all plausible conjectures in matters of historical investigation should be subjected to the most rigorous of tests before being advanced to the dignity of working hypotheses, and my present purpose is to put Mr Oliphant's theory thoroughly to the proof. To avoid doing him a primary injustice, however, I must needs refrain from defining its characteristics at the outset, since, in order to understand exactly how it has been deduced, it is necessary that scholars should be reminded of certain details regarding early theatrical customs and the official regulation of the drama whose import few even of our finest Elizabethan experts have completely grasped.

Plays enjoyed no runs in Shakespeare's day. It is seriously to be doubted if the most successful and best acclaimed production of his time had as much as two successive performances. The custom was to give a well-received new play or popular revival intermittently throughout the season, so long as its powers of attraction lasted. Where there were no signs of a diminishing interest in a new play, it might be carried over into the ensuing season, and given in all twenty-five or thirty performances. It was then laid on the shelf for a period of a lustrum or thereabouts, after which it was deemed suitable for reproduction. But it was seldom that a revived play had all the characteristics of its original presentation, since it had become customary early in the century to give an old piece some of its pristine attractiveness by submitting it to a course of furbishing and re-topicalisation. To such an extent did this system of revision come to be practised that it was evidently deemed requisite by the Master of the Revels, who was the official licenser, that before revival the play should be submitted to him a second time. Fees for licensing were probably charged from about 1581, and there is no reason to doubt that for a considerable period, extending to a quarter of a century and probably more, licences were permanent. Precisely when relicensing on revival was insisted upon is indeterminable, but there are some grounds for thinking it was delayed until Sir Henry Herbert's accession to office in 1623. Astley then farmed out the Mastership of the Revels to Herbert for £150 a year, an arrangement which, seeing that Herbert had to make £3 a week before gaining any profit, necessitated an advance of rates and the imposition of new exactions upon the players. In the beginning, however, Herbert reallowed several old plays without fee, no alterations having been made, the licences being required because the allowed copies had been lost. But his books show that on July 7, 1624, he charged ten shillings "for the adding of a scene to *The Virgin Martyr*", and on May 13, 1629, a like fee "for allowing of a new act in an ould play", the property of an unnamed company. Though both entries indicate revivals, we have as yet no clue to the charging of a fee for revival *qua* revival, whether or no any revision or radical alteration of the play had been made. That system, however, was eventually adopted, and Herbert, whose fee for licensing a new play was £2, came to demand half that sum for reallowing an old one. On October 18, 1633, at a period when some unauthorised offensive matter had been added to *The Woman's Prize, or The Tamer*

AN   12

Tamed by the King's Men on its revival, an act of contumacy which occasioned his interference, he wrote in his Office Book, as if transcribing a mandate to the transgressors:

All ould plays ought to bee brought to the master of the Revells, and have his allowance to them, for which he should have his fee, since they may be full of offensive things against church and state; ye rather that in former time the poetts tooke greater liberty than is allowed them by mee.[1]

This was Joseph Surface's morality. Herbert could not have been held responsible for the laxity of his predecessors, and it is plain to be seen that his real anxiety was about his fees. In this connexion, it is noteworthy that the first record we have of his charging £1 for reallowing an old play with alterations occurs two months earlier, or on August 15, when he relicensed *Hymen's Holiday* for the Cockpit players. Whatever the warning given to the King's Men, they evidently took it to heart, for on November 23 following, Herbert notes the receipt from them of his regulation fee for the perusal and allowance, after some reformations, of Fletcher's *The Loyal Subject*, a play originally licensed by Bucke in 1618, taking particular care to

[1] J. Q. Adams, *The Dramatic Records of Sir Henry Herbert*, pp. 20–1.

append marginally that this was "the first ould play" formally submitted to him by the company. The fact that these players had not for ten years previously sent in anything for relicensing leaves room for the assumption that relicensing on revival was not a recognised principle when Herbert succeeded to office, and had not become regularised, despite sundry small payments for additions, until some years later.

We have no further record of the master's receipt of twenty shillings for reallowing an old play for the King's Men before September 16, 1635, on which date the usual fee was paid by them "for renewing *Love's Pilgrimage*". But there must have been other entries of the sort in the interim, and the fact that they are lacking is a painful reminder of Malone's and Chalmers's absurd selectiveness in transcribing items from the Revels Office Books, as if there were any details therein unworthy of preservation. Perhaps one should have said here publishing instead of transcribing, for the evidence is that Malone made a complete transcript of the books, which, like the originals, afterwards disappeared. We know, however, that on August 16, 1634, Herbert received a fee for reallowing "an ould play, with some new scenes, *Doctor Lambe and the Witches*, to Salisbury Court", evidently a stale piece with a new title brought out in opposition to the Globe production of *The Late Lancashire Witches*. That this practice was not uncommon in late Caroline days is shown by Herbert's entry of May 12, 1636: "Received of ould Cartwright for allowing the company to add scenes to an ould play, and to give it out for a new one...£1." Its existence throws a grim light on Herbert's character and indicates that he was not above compounding with dishonesty, when he was paid for it. To give an old play with a new title without the Master of the Revels' authority would have been equivalent to performing an unlicensed play, since licences were written on the last page of the playhouse script and had to be produced on demand. Hence the proceeding would not have been without a certain measure of risk.

It is a nice question how long the relicensing of an old play held good. My impression is that it remained valid just as long as the licensees kept the play alive in their repertory, and that, with the lapse of a season in which it was wholly unrepresented, a fresh licence would be required for its further performance. This is pure assumption, but it is borne out by later evidence. With his reinstatement as Master of the Revels at the Restoration, Herbert succeeded in imposing his old charges upon the players and insisted on all old plays being relicensed on the old terms. It sounds astonishing, but we have actual evidence that in 1663–4 he received fees at the rate of £1 for reallowing *The Taming of the Shrew*, *Macbeth* and *Henry VIII*.[1]

Armed with these details, we are now in a position to comprehend on what Mr Oliphant's theory relative to the origin and significance of the double play-title is based. Mr Oliphant believes that, where we find it, the double title is "an almost sure sign that the play concerned has known revival, and probably rewriting". His assumption is that most plays were retitled on revival, and that plays eventually came to have double titles cumulatively, on publication, through the fusion of the first and second titles. The objection to this is that the manuscript from which the play was printed is most likely to have borne a single title only, not both. A safer assumption in accord with the theory would be that a combination of titles took place on the second revival of the play. That this might have happened occasionally is not improbable, but the possible instances are not sufficiently numerous to warrant the conclusion that the double title had its origin in a cumulative way. It is impolitic, therefore, to assume (as Mr Oliphant does), that any particular

[1] J. Q. Adams, *Dramatic Records*, p. 138.

double title has historical significance. The truth of the matter is that the double title can be shown to have been reached early in the seventeenth century by easy transition, and not circuitously. In this connexion one requires to bear in mind that compound titles were not peculiar to English drama, that they were given in France to several of the early plays of Hardi, and were much affected a little later by such writers as Rotrou, Scudery, Desfontaines and Scarron. Though no question of influence arises, there was a certain analogy in usage between the two countries: in both the first title was commonly of a distinctive, unmeaning order, and the second descriptive.

When we seek for proof that with us the double title did not originate in a cumulative way, we find it abundantly enough in certain early plays printed shortly after their production, and considerably before any period of possible revival. There can be little doubt that *Cynthia's Revels*, Jonson's greeting to the new century, had from the beginning a compound title, but what it precisely then was is a puzzle. In the entry on the Stationers' Register of 1601, the play is styled *Narcissus the fountaine of self love*, on the quarto *The Fountaine of Selfe-love. Or Cynthia's Revels*, and in the folio *Cynthia's Revels or the Fountayne of Selfe-love*. In all probability, the folio gives the correct form: one recalls that in the induction to the play, the Third Child says, in allusion to the presence of a title-board, "First, the title of the play is Cynthia's Revels, as any man that hath hope to be saved by his book can witness". Nor can there be any doubt about the original naming of Jonson's ensuing, quickly published play, *Poetaster, or The Arraignment*, though both the entry on the Stationers' Register and the folio read "his" for "the", since Envy's reference in the third line of the induction (another proof of the provision of a title-board) demonstrates the accuracy of the quarto. Other double titles of the period are *Blurt Master Constable, or The Spaniard's Night Walk* (1602), *The Wonder of Women, or Sophonisba* (1606), and *Parasitaster or the Fawne* (1606). Because all these five plays happen to have been private-theatre productions, it would be idle to premise that the compound title was of a private-theatre origin. There is reason to believe that compound titles had been given to public-theatre plays somewhat earlier than to private-theatre plays. Their origin seems to have been associated with the Chronicle History, a type of play not favoured by the early private-theatre audience. That point will be discussed later, but meanwhile it is necessary to lay some emphasis on the fact that printed title-pages do not always afford accurate testimony concerning the names borne by plays either on their original production or their revival. At least one old play has come down to us by a title which, theatrically speaking, it never bore. This piece, after being entered on the Stationers' Register in 1601 by the name given it in Henslowe's Diary at the time of its composition, fell from the press belatedly, in 1616, as "English-Men for my Money: or a pleasant Comedy *Called* A Woman will haue her Wil". As the phrasing of the title-page indicates, "Englishmen for my Money"—a proverbial saying—was simply, though appositely enough, added on publication.[1] There is here, of course, no analogy with the case of *A Yorkshire Tragedy*, which, in the quarto of 1608 had for its heading, "All's One, or One of the Four Plaies in one, Called A Yorkshire Tragedy", because the piece was merely part of a composite play of uncertain title, possibly running to no more than "All's One". In plays of this curious order (seeing that in those days no programmes were provided), it seems highly probable that a fresh title-board was exposed on the stage immediately before the performance of each of its component parts.

---

[1] Not but that proverbial titles were common enough at the time of the play's production: e.g. *All's Well that Ends Well*, *The Blind eats many a Fly*, *All is not Gold that Glisters*, etc.

The occasional falsification of the names of plays in the printing counts among those snags whose unravelling renders the task of the historical investigator so difficult. In at least one instance where the act has escaped detection, scholarship has lost its bearings. There has been a tendency to identify Heywood's *The Four Prentises of London* with the lost *Godfrey of Bulloigne, with the Conquest of Jerusalem* of 1594, somewhat to the antedating of Heywood's career. But, as it happens, the original prologue was printed with the play, and in it we find one of the three speakers, whose office it is to defend the author and explain his intentions, expounding the title, which he gives as *True and Strange, or The Four Prentises of London*. This type of introduction, an amalgamation of induction and prologue, was Ben Jonson's creation, and came into brief vogue in 1599, a circumstance which helps to date Heywood's play. Out of respect for the reader's patience, I refrain from expatiating now upon the point, but some day I hope to advance cogent reasons for my belief that *True and Strange* was originally produced by Worcester's Men at the Curtain in 1601.

Concerning another public-theatre play of this period, *Twelfe Night, or What You Will*, if Mr Oliphant were to claim that the compound title was arrived at by accretion, one would have difficulty in confuting him. Since clashes in play-naming were avoided, it seems hardly likely that Marston would have written a *What You Will* close to the period of Shakespeare's comedy. Possibly, however, that difficulty would disappear were we acquainted with the dates of both pieces. Though first printed in 1607, Marston's comedy is generally, and, I think, correctly, assigned to 1601. In despite of this apparent clash, it might reasonably be argued that the full title of Shakespeare's play as we now have it was necessary in the beginning for its understanding. The bills seemingly invited the passer-by to come and see something of the nature of a holiday frolic. (Vague titles of the sort—e.g. *Look About You*— were much indulged in at the close of the sixteenth century.) Accretion in this case, if not wholly negatived, is certainly argued against by the curious circumstance that the play in later Jacobean days was known, and probably billed, as *Malvolio*. Leonard Digges, in his lines "Upon Master William Shakespeare", written in 1623, but not published until 1640, calls it by that name, and Sir Henry Herbert, in his revels records of 1623, states that "at Candlemas *Malvolio* was acted at court, by the king's servants". Moreover, the title has been so altered in Charles I's copy of the Second Folio.

Since, as we have seen, the double title cannot have

been arrived at *ab initio* by accretion, we are forced to follow Mr Oliphant's example, and speculate as to its origin. Titles of the sort were so seldom given to book or pamphlet in the late sixteenth century that one cannot safely affirm it was due to the adoption by one class of authors of another class's practice. Rather would it appear to be a natural transition from a title so diffuse as to be clumsy to a title of compactness, somewhat less descriptive. In the billing of Chronicle Histories, it had been a common, but not unvaried, practice to catch the eye of the wayfarer with a trick title, set out in bold type, and then convey to him some particulars of the proffered play. As an example of "the long-tayled title", to quote Nash's phrase, one may cite (despite its avoidance of the catch heading) the title given in the First Quarto of 1 *Henry IV*, which reads: "The History of Henrie the Fourth; With the battell at Shrewsburye betweene the King & Lord Henry Percy, surnamed Hotspur of the North. With the humorous conceits of Sir John Falstaffe". Here, as in other instances of the sort, the title-page undoubtedly followed the wording of the playbill. It is never good policy to overcrowd a poster, and, for the very good reason that they were stuck on posts, posters in Shakespeare's day were small. Hence, we have only to postulate a growing tendency towards concision to arrive at the origin of the double title. Neatness in nomenclature was, however, a thing of slow attainment. The title-page of Dekker's *The Shoemaker's Holiday* in the quarto of 1600, shortly after the play's production, reads in part, "The Shoemaker's Holiday. Or the Gentle Craft. With the humorous Life of Simon Eyre, shoemaker, and Lord Maior of London". *The Gentle Craft*, it may be noted, was the name of Deloney's tract from which the dramatist derived his theme: a delicate way of making acknowledgment. But in the course of a lustrum even the writers of Chronicle Histories had attained the knack of crisp titling, e.g. Heywood's *If You Know not me, You Know no bodie: or The Troubles of Queene Elizabeth.* It is curious, however, to note that in the Second Part of the play there was evidence of back-sliding, since the title ran: *If You Know not me, you know no bodie. With the Building of the Royal Exchange: And the famous Victorie of Queene Elizabeth in the Yeare* 1588. For the older type of dramatist, the old Adam proved too strong. Even so late as 1610 or thereabouts we find Webster combining the two methods in *The White Divel; Or, The Tragedy of Paulo Giordano Ursini, Duke of Brachiano, With the Life and Death of Vittoria Corombona the famous Venetian Curtizan.* But one is apt to suspect that now and again extra descriptive matter was added to the title on publication.

It is curious that the catch-title should have been peculiarly associated with, and almost the prerogative of, the Chronicle History. A further example besides those already given is Rowley's *When You See Me, You Know Me. Or The Famous Chronicle Historie of King Henry the Eight, with the birth and vertuous life of Edward Prince of Wales*. This long-popular play, which first fell from the press in 1605, is chiefly memorable for the fact that its renewed vogue inspired the writing of Shakespeare's *Henry VIII*: a fact of which we get abundant proof not only in the arrogant prologue to the Globe play but in its real title. It was called *All is True*, in disparagement of the alluring falsity of most of the incidents in Rowley's play; and its full title, if one may deduce by analogy, was, in all probability, something like "*All is True, or The Real Chronicle History of King Henry the Eighth*".

In the days when there were no programmes to preserve and no newspapers to discuss theatrical events, the playgoer gave short shrift to a long title and generally recalled a popular piece in a familiar way, by something easily rememberable. And, when the hour of revival came, the players generally fell in line. Thus second titles often triumphed over first. *Volpone* came to be acted as *The Fox*, *Epicoene* as *The Silent Woman*, *Othello* as *The Moore of Venice*, and *The Woman's Prize* as *The Tamer Tamed*. But caprice often ruled in these matters, and it is sometimes difficult to divine how a play derived its second and final title in cases where it had only one in the beginning. Here is perhaps the most baffling example. On May 11, 1633, Herbert licensed a posthumous comedy of Fletcher's as *The Night Walkers*, the precise name under which it was played at Court in the following January, and entered on the Stationers' Register in April 1639, save that in the latter instance the title was in the singular. But when the play came to be printed in 1640 it was called *The Night Walker, or The Little Thief*, and when revived at the Restoration it was known only by its subtitle. Doubtless there is some playing here to Mr Oliphant's hand. Accretion cannot be denied, and the only question is how it came about. It would appear as if the play had been produced under its licensed title and given an entirely new title on its revival *circa* 1638. But to take this view is to assume that it had never been acted under its double title, and that the fusion took place on publication. In one particular case where the double title was certainly accretive, the second title was unknown and unutilised before the printing of the play.

Heywood's *Love's Mistress; or The Queen's Masque* was originally produced at the Cockpit under its first title in 1634, and acquired its second on publication two years later in commemoration of the fact that the play had been very much liked by the Queen, and had been acted at Court three times within a brief period.

Sometimes the process was reversed. A play of Massinger's, licensed as *The Renegado, or The Gentleman of Venice* in April 1624, for the Cockpit, was published in 1630 simply as *The Renegado*. Occasionally there is curious variation. In the first four quartos of the play (the fourth in 1648), *The Woman Hater* is so styled *tout court*, but in the fifth (issued by the publisher of the fourth in 1649) it is given the alternative title "Or the Hungry Courtier". This last quarto has a prologue by Davenant, originally published in his *Madagascar* in 1638, and undoubtedly written for a revival of the play a little before that date. Most likely it was at this period, when double titles were much in vogue, that Beaumont's old comedy acquired its secondary designation.

In dealing with Caroline times, it is important to bear in mind that Herbert's entries are not always sound—sometimes they are merely confusing—evidence on the question of original titling. In October 1632, he records the receipt of a licensing fee for *Humours Reconcil'd, or The Magnetick Lady*, a reversal of the titles only to be clearly detected by a reference to Ben Jonson's induction. Damplay's questions to the boy, after gazing on the title-board, plainly indicate that the name of the unfortunate play on its production was identical with the name given it on publication.

Perhaps the main characteristic of theatrical procedure in the first half of the seventeenth century was the servile deference to public opinion. There was no persisting then with the performance of a *Playboy of the Western World* once there had been a general turning down of thumbs. In the matter of play-titles, dramatists proposed and the public disposed. As I have already shown, popular acclaim ordained it that many plays should become established under their subtitles, or, as might be likewise argued, under some name bestowed upon them from without. *The Humorous Lieutenant* is a typical example. There has come down to us a scrivener's transcript of this long popular play, made in 1625, about five years after its production, in which the title is given as *Demetrius and Enanthe*. It would appear that originally the piece was called *Demetrius and Enanthe, or The Humorous Lieutenant*, and that despite its subsequent revival as *The Noble Enemies*, the public persisted in calling it by the character that had taken its fancy, with the result that Moseley, on first printing it after the downfall of the playhouses, bowed to popular usage and simply styled it *The Humorous Lieutenant*. Times have changed. The player is now a law unto himself: the public is no longer the divinity that shapes his ends, and he rough-hews them as he pleases.

Chapter XIV

MASSINGER'S PUNCTUATION AND
WHAT IT REVEALS

It is not at all surprising that the theory boldly advanced for some time past by more than one notable Elizabethan scholar that Shakespeare's punctuation of his plays was much more rhetorical than syntactic has failed to win acceptance from cautious and slow-going investigators of the type of the late Dr R. M. Alden. Too much has been taken for granted: in our present state of knowledge, not all the premisses of the argument are sound. Before we can safely deduce Shakespeare's method of pointing from the trustworthy quartos, we shall have to determine what was the common attitude of the early seventeenth-century printers towards dramatic manuscripts, whether it was their habit, so far as the exigencies of setting up permitted, meticulously to follow copy, where the copy was fairly well punctuated, or whether the matter was treated in accord with some common principle of their own. Shakespeare cannot be viewed wholly apart on this point, and, even if we concede that the dramatists of his time adopted a practice of rhetorical punctuation, there must have been, in the composing-room, some clashing of methods.

As things stand, however, on the present lines of argument and viewing the insufficiency of data, no determination can possibly be achieved. Relief from the existing deadlock can only be attained by the procurement of analogies. The possibilities on this score have not hitherto been suspected, but it chances that a playhouse copy of a play by a noted Elizabethan dramatist, in his own hand, has come down to us, and that the manuscript betrays a certain method of restricted pointing peculiar to its author. So far as we can find traces of this distinctive punctuation in the early printed plays of the same author, just so far are we justified in concluding that the play-printers of his time followed copy. The manuscript in question is that of Massinger's *Believe as You List*, a King's Men's play of 1631, and its characteristics can readily be grasped by all scholars, far and wide, either by reference to Farmer's facsimile or to the careful type-reproduction given under Professor C. J. Sisson's supervision in the Malone Society series. My main purpose now is to show what the testing of the whole of the Massinger quartos by the light of his distinctive (if restricted) punctuation reveals, though a secondary matter of

very considerable interest will afterwards be discussed. In the manuscript, this distinctiveness is
confined to Massinger's own particular stage directions, both running and marginal, and it consists,
more especially where a sequence of names occurs,
in the use of full stops where normally commas
would be placed (e.g. "Enter Prurias. Queene.
Philoxenus."). It is mostly to be remarked in
entrance-directions at the opening of scenes, and it
is also to be noted that, not content with these
severances, either Massinger or the prompter has,
in some cases, drawn short perpendicular lines
between the names of characters as well. Of this
curious pointing there are, in all, fifteen examples
in the manuscript (see the Malone Society reproduction, pp. 3, 20, 25, 40, 44, 46, 47 (margin), 49,
56 (margin), 63, 65 (margin), 66 (margin), 75, 86,
87 (margin)).

While, in the majority of the Massinger quartos,
sporadic instances of this peculiarity are to be found,
it is plain to be seen that towards Massinger's unique
pointing of stage directions the printers preserved
no consistency of attitude. For our present purpose,
it is convenient to divide the quartos into two
sections, those published during Massinger's lifetime, and those published within a score of years
after. Of the four belated quartos, three—*The*

Guardian, The Bashful Lover and *A Very Woman*, all issued together in 1655—afford no inkling of Massinger's individual pointing. Equally innocent of all abnormality of the sort are *The Duke of Milan* of 1623 (notable as Massinger's first printed play) and *The Roman Actor* of 1629. In regard to the former this is surprising, seeing that the piece was a recent production and that the text was derived from a playhouse copy. But in all the remaining nine quartos (reckoning only those whose authorship is solely attributed to Massinger), either instances of his peculiar pointing are to be found or traces of its influence are to be suspected. In *The Bondman* of 1624, there are three examples, one at the opening of act I, sc. 3, one medially in the same scene, and one at the opening of the third act. In the earliest of these instances, it is plain to be seen that the compositor halted between two opinions, since he set up the direction partly in Massinger's way and partly in his own. It reads, "Archidamus Cleon. Diphilus, Olimpia. Corisca, Cleora. Zanthia." Other printers, equally nonplussed by Massinger's heteronomous pointing, compromised in different ways. Some solved the puzzle by omitting intermediate stops, as in *The Picture* quarto of 1630, wherein we get, at the opening of act III, sc. 2, "Enter Sophia Corisca." Others softened Massinger's full stops

13-3

into colons, as in *The Unnatural Combat* of 1639, which confronts us in its fifth act with, "Enter Beaufort senior: Beaufort junior: Montague: Chamont: Lanour: Belgarde: Montreville: Soldiers." Earlier in the same play, however, in the second act, Massinger's influence is more clearly to be traced in "Enter Beaufort jun. Montreville. Belgarde, the three Sea Captaines."

But of all the Massinger quartos, undoubtedly the most important from our present standpoint is the *New Way to Pay Old Debts* of 1633, inasmuch as, for once in a while, it indicates a careful following of copy throughout. Not only are the directions for entries at its scene openings disfigured with intermediate periods, but mid-scene examples are to be found in act III, sc. 4 and act IV, sc. 1, and one actually occurs in the first mentioned scene in an "exeunt". In all the other quartos, however, in which abnormally punctuated directions occur, inconsistency flaunts itself at the scene openings. In *The Maid of Honour*, as printed from a prompt copy in 1632, Massinger's eccentric pointing is faithfully followed in the initial directions of act I, sc. 1, act II, sc. 4 and 5, act IV, sc. 4 and 5, act V, sc. 1 and 2, but not at all in the third act save once medially. Similarly, in *The Emperor of the East*, printed in the same year and likewise from a prompt copy, directions of the type under discussion are to be found only at the openings of act I, sc. I, and act III, sc. 1, 2, 3, and 4. So, too, in *The Great Duke of Florence* quarto of 1636, there are Massinger-stopped directions at the outset of act I, sc. I, act II, sc. 2 and act III, sc. I, but none elsewhere save one medially in act II, sc. 2. But the puzzlement of the compositors was, apparently, at its severest at an earlier period. In *The Renegado* of 1630, we get a typical Massinger direction at the opening of act I, sc. 2, but in act II, sc. 5, after starting the scene in true Massingerian style with "Enter Aga. Capi-aga.", the setter went off at a tangent and finished up with a sequence of commas. One has no doubt, moreover, that later on (in act IV, sc. 2) Massinger is lurking behind the direction, "Enter Asambeg. unlocks the doore. leades forth Paulina." One notes, by the way, that some of the instructions for entrance in this play have (sensibly enough, of course) medial full stops in association with con-tracted names, and wonders whether the compositor simply followed copy or was prompted to make the contractions to justify the irritating full stops. Even to the last the puzzlement never wholly ceased. It is true, as already stated, that in setting up three out of the four Massinger quartos issued during the Inter-regnum, the printers blandly cut the Gordian knot by ignoring Massinger's aberrations. Yet in the

fourth, *The City Madam* of 1658, last of all to fall
from the press, there are medially in act v, sc. 1, two
glaring examples of corrupted Massinger which
to the initiated speak eloquently of some poor
printer's disquietude.

It is not to be expected that this punctuation test
will apply to Massinger's collaborated work, either
known or suspected. While there is good reason to
believe that in the case of early plays of single
authorship, the author made his own fair copy for
theatrical use, on the other hand, in the case of
collaborated work, the evidence is that the authors'
foul sheets were delivered to the players and uni-
fication effected by transcription by an expert hand,
either a stage official or a scrivener. But, perplexingly
enough, while this conclusion is borne out by the
belated quarto of *The Old Law* (1656), which yields
no slightest trace of Massinger's direction-pointing,
it is seemingly traversed by the significance of three
directions in *The Fatal Dowry* (1652). All are mid-
scene, not opening, directions, and in two of them
(one in act I, sc. 1 and one in act II, sc. 1) colons are
placed between the names instead of full stops, as if
the compositor had boggled over his copy and
decided to meet Massinger half-way. One could
perhaps afford to ignore these suspicions were it not
for the fact that earlier in act II, sc. 1, is to be found

a long direction highly reminiscent of Massinger's style. It runs: "Enter Funerall. Body borne by 4. Captaines and Souldiers. Mourners, Scutcheons, and very good order. Charalois. and Romont meet it. Char. speaks, Rom. weeping, solemne Musique. 3 Creditors." (It is noteworthy that the first three full stops in the direction are larger than the others and oddly diamond-shaped.) Infiltrations by the prompter are here to be suspected, and, assuming the prompter to have been the maker of the playhouse copy, it may be that in this case he largely preserved Massinger's punctuation while augmenting the particulars for stage purposes.

Taken in the mass, the foregoing details point to a lack of system in the composing-room of the earlier part of the seventeenth century, and are eloquent of the difficulties which must be surmounted before there can be determination of the main characteristics of Shakespeare's pointing. But it remains to be shown that all the possibilities of the test have not been exhausted. It can be applied to the many plays of Fletcher in which Massinger's revising hand has long been suspected. But, in this connexion, a word of caution is necessary. The presence of a Massinger-like direction in a Fletcher play is fairly indicative of Massinger's revision of the play for a revival, but the absence of all such directions cannot be taken to prove the contrary, seeing that Massinger may have revised the text without tampering with the stage directions.

My own experience may prove instructive. On careful examination of the Beaumont and Fletcher First Folio, I find that six of Fletcher's plays as there given betray Massinger's hand in the directions. The strongest evidence is in *The Custom of the Country* which affords thirteen examples (act II, sc. I, opening, "Enter Manuell du Sosa. and Guiomar."; act III, sc. I, opening; act V, sc. I, *passim*, eleven instances, including "Enter Mannuel Charino. Arnaldo, Zenocia, borne in a chaire. 2 Doctors. Clodio." and "Enter. Hypollita. leading Leopold. Arnoldo. Zenocia. In either hand. Zabulon. Sulpitia."). Most investigators take this to be a Fletcher-Massinger play, the result of collaboration, but the evidence yielded by the direction test indicates Massinger simply as a reviser. With the exception of act III, sc. I, Oliphant[1] attributes all the scenes in which the above-mentioned directions occur to Massinger: admirable detective work.

Next in importance comes *Beggar's Bush*, in which there are eight Massinger-like directions, all presenting incongruous full stops (act III, sc. 3, opening,

[1] In his indispensable book, *The Plays of Beaumont and Fletcher*, to which the references are throughout.

"Enter. Vandunck, Hubert. Hemskirck. and Margaret. Boores."; act III, sc. I, one medially; act III, sc. 3, two examples, the first of which reads, "Enter Higgen. Prig, Ferret. Gynks. and the rest of the Boores."; act III, sc. 4, opening; act IV, sc. I, one at opening and one later; act IV, sc. 3, one medially). This play was produced in 1622, and revived in 1636. It bears signs of clumsy revision, and a variant text is to be found in the Second Folio. Most investigators attribute it to Fletcher and Massinger. Oliphant finds traces of Massinger's hand in the first, second and fifth acts only, adding "M.'s insertions in II, 3 and V, I, are very characteristic of his methods as a reviser".

In *The Double Marriage* there are few directions that one can bring oneself to attribute to Massinger. Now and again there is a curious use of "En." for "Enter", but, all told, there are only two directions which, by any stretching, could be deemed his. These occur in act III, sc. I, and read: (*a*) "Flourish colours.[1] En. Castruccio like the King, in the midst of a gard. Villio."; (*b*) "Enter Ferand. Rouvere." Still, investigators may be right in seeing traces of Massinger in the play. Boyle gives the whole of act III, sc. I to his pen, but Oliphant, the more perceptive critic, finds him only in the second half of

[1] Evidently a misprint of "cornets".

the scene, indicating that his is a revising, not a collaborating hand.

In *The Little French Lawyer* the only smack of Massinger's punctuation to be found occurs in act IV, sc. I, in a direction reading, "Enter Vertaigne Chambernell. Beaupre, Verdoone, Lamira, Annabell. Charlote, Nurse." Here, surely, we have a printer's paltering with heterodoxy. The play has been unanimously assigned by the critics to Fletcher and Massinger. It is odd that Oliphant should assign act IV, sc. I to Fletcher, but his division of the work constitutes Massinger simply a reviser.

Little is known about *The Noble Gentleman*. It was licensed in 1626, shortly after Fletcher's death, for the King's Men, and exists only in a sadly corrupt form. The chances are that it was left unfinished, and completed by another hand. No one has suggested that Massinger was in any wise associated with it, but, here and there, there are slight indications of his trail, or a trail suspiciously like his. Thus, at the opening of the second act we get, "Enter. Gentleman Solus.", and at the opening of act IV, "Enter Cozen. his Wife.", and later on in the latter-mentioned scene comes, "Enter Jaques. In womens aparrell."

In two other plays with which Massinger is thought to have been associated, *The Fair Maid of*

the Inn and *The Knight of Malta*, one finds little to go upon. But it may be that the opening direction in the former was again a printer's compromise. It runs, "Ent. Duke of Florence. Alberto: Baptista: Magistrates And Attendants." One would hardly be disposed to draw attention to this, were it not for the fact that Cruikshank assigns the opening scene of the play, and Boyle and Oliphant give the whole of the first act, to Massinger. A like incertitude attaches itself to a medial direction in act IV, sc. I of *The Knight of Malta*, which reads, "Exeunt. En. Rocca Mountferrat Abdilla. With a dark lanthorn.";
but here lack of pointing between the names seems once more to hint at a compositor's bewilderment and hesitation. One, however, is encouraged to advance so doubtful an item by the circumstance that most investigators are of the opinion that Massinger revised the play, and that so discriminating a critic as Oliphant finds traces of him in this very scene.

Finally, it needs to be said that in certain of the plays included in the First Folio in which delvers into the Beaumont and Fletcher mine believe they have discovered Massingerian ore, no trace occurs of Massinger's direction-pointing. Happily, no one's withers are wrung by this assertion, for, in these cases, negative evidence is none.

INDEX

Henry VIII, 101, 121, 181, 189
Henslowe, Philip, 11, 15, 90, 184
Hentzner, Paul, 1
Herbert, Sir Henry, 177, 180, 186, 190, 191
Heywood, Thomas, 6, 12, 24, 25, 86, 120, 121, 156, 185, 188, 191
Hillebrand, Professor H. N., 28, 34 note, 35 note
Historical Register for the Year 1736, 151
Histriomastix, 14
Home, John, 112
Honor Military and Civil, 145 note
Hood, 57
Hotson, Leslie, 51 note
Houghton, Lord, 58
Hour Glass, The, 89
Humorous Lieutenant, The, 192, 193
Humours Reconcil'd, 192
Hunnis, William, 37
Hymen's Holiday, 178

If It be not Good, the Divel is in It, 92, 95
If You Know not me, You Know no bodie, 12, 188
Ignoramus, or the Academical Lawyer, 51
Interlude of Youth, The, 115
Irish Fine Lady, The, 152
Iron Age, The, 121
Irving, Henry, 58, 96
Irving, Washington, 126

James I, 41
Jew of Malta, 85
John, King, 86
Jones, Inigo, 132, 134, 143
Jonson, Ben, 3, 4, 12, 14, 47, 119, 132, 134, 136, 137, 141–7, 183, 185, 192

Kean, Edmund, 122
Killigrew, Tom, 46
King's Men, the, 26, 42, 101, 178, 179, 195, 204
King's Playhouse, 46
Kinsky, George, 91 note
Knight of Malta, The, 205
Kyd, Thomas, 38

Lamb, Charles, 113
Lanier, Nicolas, 141
Late Lancashire Witches, 24, 25, 180
Lear, King, 73, 79
Lee, Mrs Mary, 81
Lee, Nathaniel, 81
Lee, Sir Henry, 145 note
Linley, Thomas, 55, 56
Little Ark of Seventeenth Century Verse, A, 108 note
Little French Lawyer, The, 204
Little Thief, The, 190
Locrine, 12, 26, 60
Look About You, 23, 186
Lord's Masque, The, 133, 139, 141, 143
Love in a Maze, 148
Love in a Village, 113
Lovers Made Men, 141
Love's Mistress, 191
Love's Pilgrimage, 179
Loyal Subject, The, 119 note, 178
Lusty Juventus, 115
Lyceum Theatre, 128
Lying Lover, The, 150
Lyly, John, 38

Macbeth, 10, 17, 21, 22, 75, 85, 87–9, 181
Macklin, Charles, 152
Magnetick Lady, The, 192
Mahon, Robert, 111
Maid of Honour, The, 50, 198

CAMBRIDGE: PRINTED BY W. LEWIS, M.A., AT THE UNIVERSITY PRESS